a Diary of
REVIVAL

0-8054-3195-0

Published by Broadman & Holman Publishers
Nashville, Tennessee

Published in 2004 in Great Britain by CWR under the same title

Dewey Decimal Classification: 269.24
Subject Heading: REVIVALS \ RELIGIOUS AWAKENING—WALES

1 2 3 4 5 6 7 8 9 10 10 09 08 07 06 05 04

KEVIN ADAMS

a Diary of

REVIVAL

THE OUTBREAK OF THE 1904 WELSH AWAKENING

BROADMAN
& HOLMAN
PUBLISHERS

Nashville, Tennessee

To Gwenfair

CONTENTS

FOREWORD

The year 2004 has witnessed a number of celebrations in the nation of Wales as, from one end of the Principality to the other, Christians remember the great spiritual revival that took place one hundred years ago under the charismatic young preacher Evan Roberts. Centenary meetings have been arranged, books produced, and many sections of the media have reported on what happened when in the fall of 1904 Wales was visited by a great outpouring of the Spirit—an event that changed the entire face of the nation. Amidst all these celebrations, nothing, I believe, is more significant than the publication of this book, *A Diary of Revival,* written by Kevin Adams.

In many ways the book is unique in that it contains information that hitherto has not been available to the Christian public. Its chief distinction, however, is that largely it lets Evan Roberts tell his own story by threading together his personal thoughts and feelings as he moved through that great and wonderful time.

Kevin is not only an historian and a researcher but a passionate advocate for revival and a great believer in the fact that what God did one hundred years ago He is able to do again. Rarely have I met anyone who carries such a burden for revival and whose enthusiasm for the subject shines through in almost everything he says and does. He makes clear that a twenty-first-century revival may well have different features to what took place a hundred years ago when society was quite different, but the common denominator in all revival throughout history is an awesome sense of God's presence felt not only by those who attend church but by those also in the outside community.

My hope as you read this book—and I am sure it is Kevin's too—is that you will not only glean more information on what God did in those distant and far off days but that you will lay hold of Him in prayer and plead with Him to open the heavens and give us a visitation of His Spirit that will touch every nation on the face of the earth.

I hope you will enjoy as I have this "feast of good things."

Selwyn Hughes
LIFE PRESIDENT
Crusade for World Revival (CWR)

ACKNOWLEDGMENTS

A special thank you to Molly Pegram, Daniela Ragsdale, Cerys Morgan, Carys Davies, Jan Lashley, Bethan Rees and Elin Anne Partridge for typing the manuscript.

I also want to express my appreciation to all the staff at CWR who worked with me on this book.

INTRODUCTION

Revival is a word and concept increasingly in the thoughts and aspirations of twenty-first-century Christians around the globe. While past revivals are read about and studied in the West, in many parts of the world they are a present reality, where thousands are committing themselves for the first time to Christ, and others are finding a renewed vigour and reality in their personal faith as they experience an intensification of the Holy Spirit's work in their midst.

Yet for many in the West the last 100 years have been years of spiritual decline and evangelistic frustration. A serious decrease in church attendance has threatened to leave the Church as a seemingly irrelevant remnant of a bygone age, tolerated or patronised by a society that claims to have moved on to greater things. And as Christians view the ever-darkening spiritual forecast, a temptation just to give up and despair can easily further paralyse the already weakened churches. This book is written in the belief that the God of history past is also the God of history present, not only in far-away societies but also in the rugged present of twenty-first-century life. It is written in order to remind believers of what God can do through and with ordinary and extraordinary people, young and old, male and female, when they are committed to Him.

The story of these pages is not a 'magical answer' to the decline of today's Western church, one that will somehow suddenly appear like the Seventh Cavalry to the rescue of the spiritual remnant just in the nick of time. And it isn't a visitation of God unrelated to what the Church might be doing at any particular moment; not even a sudden supernatural downpour, which in a few days would cause the empty churches to be full again. I do not see it like that. Rather, this book is written to remind the Church that God uses people—real people, normal people, ordinary people, even flawed and immature people—to further His cause. It is written to encourage believers that He can still use and work through them in their situation. It is written to highlight the fact that at the beginning of the twentieth century in Wales God did just this, and although Church and society were obviously different 100 years ago, lessons and encouragements from the developing history of God working through His Church shouldn't be lost.

GOD DOES NOT BYPASS HIS CHURCH TO WORK OUT HIS PURPOSE, BUT CALLS IT TO CONFORM TO HIS WILL AND HIS PLAN.

Many have predicted and even prophesied revival in Wales in the near future. It is not for me—a mere flawed mortal—to know the day or hour, and when asked the question whether I believe He will visit again soon I point the questioner to the Sovereign God, who knows better than I. In revisiting the story of the outbreak of revival in 1904, I am reminded of the part believers themselves have to play in the growth, extension and success of God's cause. When God used a young ex-coalminer, He was using someone who *had* prayed, who *had* obeyed, who *had* been faithful, who *had* sought, who *had* got involved, who *had* put his offering on the altar. In other words, Evan Roberts was no passive instrument of supernatural power, but before and during the revival an active player in the ongoing purposes of God. His story can never be used as an excuse for doing nothing.

The story of 1904 is not a justification for inaction and passivity on the part of God's Church and people, but rather as a stimulus for God-anointed and Spirit-led action. God in His sovereign wisdom has chosen His people to be His instruments, the active and visible body of Christ in the world. God does not bypass His Church to work out His purpose, but calls it to conform to His will and His plan. The story of Evan Roberts is the struggle of one young man who dared to say, 'Thy will be done' and, as a result, saw something of 'Thy kingdom come' in Wales at the beginning of the twentieth century. The struggle that Evan Roberts underwent was not without pain and cost, and he realised that carrying the cross was a prerequisite to its effective and powerful proclamation. May his story of struggle and victory be an encouragement to others to pursue a similar course, leading again to spiritual renewal.

Evan Roberts

Evan himself still remains, for many, a controversial figure. While some early writers have been too starry-eyed to write objectively, others have let some of his faults colour the whole picture. In order that modern readers may make up their own minds, I have sought to let Evan himself do much of the talking. Taking autobiographical material from the letters that he wrote during the several weeks just previous to and during the outbreak of revival, it is possible, after 100 years, to hear Evan Roberts speak again about his hopes, his fears, his spiritual struggles and his depth of spiritual experience. It's all there in his own words, written at the time.

Most of the letters cover the period from September to November 1904, a crucial time in the development of Evan Roberts' spirituality, and also a time that covers his six-week stay at Newcastle Emlyn and his first two weeks at Moriah Chapel, Loughor. These letters, with other autobiographical material, sometimes from the newspapers of the time, give us an intimate insight into the personality of the young revivalist. They tell the story of the beginnings of the 1904 revival and the various influences on Evan himself during that period, influences that were then to colour the development of the revival throughout the winter of 1904/05. Key characteristics of the Welsh Revival—such as the emphasis on spontaneity, the Spirit's leading, prayer, open confession, the place of women and the baptism of the Spirit—all appear or are present at this time. It could be argued that this period is a microcosm of the history of the Welsh Revival, at least as far as it was led by Evan Roberts, and an understanding of the development of the revivalist's spirituality at this time casts much light on the nature of the revival itself as it spread throughout Wales in the next six months. This period highlights

 the strengths and weaknesses of the young revivalist; strengths and weaknesses that would become evident in the ensuing spread of the awakening.

In order to appreciate and follow the story, the material has been arranged chronologically, as if written in a diary format. The words are all those of the revivalist, the format is mine. Material about meetings and incidents are included under the date that they happened, although often the incident might be written about some days later. Details of dates are all noted, while feelings and thoughts are included under the date of writing, giving insight into Evan's mind and thoughts at the time of writing. Personalised material has been omitted—for example, 'Dear Syd, How are you?' etc—as this does not conform to a diary format. The original letters were written in Welsh; translations were given by D.M. Phillips in his book *Evan Roberts: The Great Welsh Revivalist and His Work* (London, Marshall Bros., 1906; eighth edn, 1923). Where words could be misunderstood, I have re-translated them from the original Welsh.

The book also contains other eyewitness accounts of the incidents recorded, enabling us to see them from other perspectives, Seth Joshua's diary being an example of this. Mini-biographies of key characters—W.W. Lewis, Evan Phillips—are included, with insight passages containing added historical or theological information relevant to the narrative where needed.

The first chapters have a more conventional biographical format and serve as an introduction to the diary, helping to place it in its cultural and historical context, while the last chapter, 'The Enigma of Evan Roberts', will seek to explain, from my perspective at least, the secret of the popularity of the revivalist.

WALES—A SPIRITUAL HISTORY

The arrival of Christianity in Wales during the first three centuries of the Christian era is shrouded in the mists of mythological speculation, due to the scarcity of written material and the vivid imagination or gullibility of medieval historians. But arrive it did, probably brought by individual Roman soldiers or merchants, in the opening centuries of the first millennium. For the first few hundred years, its introduction impacted the Roman towns; the native Welsh, it seemed, were still unreached.

Their conversion was achieved from the fifth to the seventh centuries, in a period that has become known as 'the Age of the Saints'. Again obscured by time, knowledge of this period is fragmentary. Yet we do know that a group of monastic preachers and teachers were determined to pass on the good news and to church-plant throughout the land. Leaving little physical evidence, a few hundred Celtic crosses being the most spectacular, these missionaries began the work of transforming a nation, creating centres of learning at Llantwit Major and Llancarfan, and planting hundreds of churches throughout the land. These were to become the foundation of Christian Wales.

> **FROM THE FIFTH TO THE SEVENTH CENTURIES ... KNOWN AS THE AGE OF THE SAINTS ... MISSIONARIES BEGAN THE WORK OF TRANSFORMING A NATION ...**

The Norman invasion of the eleventh century saw the building of stone churches, and the establishment of a new parish system, some more monastic establishments at Strata Florida and Llanbadarn becoming centres of learning and writing. Wales became absorbed into medieval European Christendom. The sixteenth-century Protestant Reformation, which quickly revolutionised medieval Europe under Luther and Calvin, initially made little impact on Wales. Although externally Protestant, Wales saw the new faith as English, and therefore foreign and suspect. It won over very few hearts and minds.

Of course, this period saw the translation of the Bible into the Welsh language. In 1588, the year of the Spanish Armada, the task was completed by William Morgan. It was a feat that not only saved the Welsh language and culture but impregnated them with a spiritual potential, that would bloom in years to come.

The seventeenth century saw further efforts truly to see the Welsh people come into the spiritual heritage of the Reformation. Puritan preachers, seeking a pure Church, sought to spread the gospel message, but it seemed that Wales was still not ready to enter the promised land.

The crossing of the Jordan came with the sudden conversion and later ministry of a few key men: Howell Harris, the zealous exhorter and preacher, converted in 1735; along with Daniel Rowland, an Anglican clergyman; and William

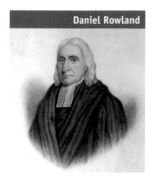

Daniel Rowland

Williams, the great hymn-writer. These spiritual pioneers became key instruments in transforming Welsh Wales. The Welsh Scriptures came alive under the preaching of Rowland, and their truth was experienced through the metaphors and brilliance of Williams' hymns, many of which became anthems of a nation that was continuing to find its spiritual feet. This enthusiasm and spiritual vitality was infectious and, by the end of the eighteenth century, the Congregationalists and Baptists, at first suspicious of the more charismatic Methodist movement, also began experiencing a newness in their worship and a restored confidence in their preaching.

The story of the nineteenth century in Wales is one of spiritual consolidation and growth, sprinkled with outbreaks of revival, large and small, national and local. These revivals were characterised by powerful preaching, intense prayer, and sometimes uninhibited worship, and they continued to give impetus to church growth and Christian influence in the nation.

By the second half of the century, Wales could, without too much exaggeration, be described as a Christian nation. The church, or increasingly the nonconformist chapel, was becoming the centre of spiritual and social life. Its influence was all-pervading. Sunday schools were well attended; even smaller churches had regular rolls of over 100. Evenings were taken up with prayer meetings and the peculiarly Welsh *Seiat* or 'experience meeting', where ordinary believers would share their spiritual ups and downs. This small-group system of mutual spiritual help and accountability was to provide a depth, as well as a breadth, for the growing numbers of believers throughout the land. On top of this, there were meetings for young people, the Band of Hope, lectures, cultural meetings, singing and preaching festivals. The nonconformist calendar could be a busy one!

> **THE CHURCH ... WAS BECOMING THE CENTRE OF SPIRITUAL AND SOCIAL LIFE ... WHERE ORDINARY BELIEVERS WOULD SHARE THEIR SPIRITUAL UPS AND DOWNS.**

During the eighteenth century, the vicar and squire had been the masters in their own communities. Increasingly during the nineteenth century the nonconformist minister was taking centre stage, winning the admiration of growing congregations with his pulpit eloquence and increasing social standing. The Scriptures were highly regarded. A literate community, due to the Sunday-school movement, learned passages by heart and respected those who helped them apply its contents. It was the period of the 'celebrity preacher', and the 'star sermon', and the respect given during the lifetime of these spiritual celebrities was often translated into a memoir or biography published soon after their demise; eulogies, sermons and letters included. And the effect was new, extended and decorated chapels, expressing in architecture and size the growing influence of evangelical Christianity during the century. The nineteenth century saw each denomination produce its periodicals and publications, commentaries, church news, missionary stories, Sunday school material and quarterly journals, all there to feed the growing interest in all things Christian. Christianity, by now, had not only landed on its feet but it was also clearly the occupying power.

> **THE RADICAL, EVANGELICAL MESSAGE OF WELSH NONCONFORMITY WAS IN DANGER OF BECOMING THE NEW CONFORMITY ...**

Yet, by the end of the nineteenth century and the beginning of the twentieth, an increasing number of people had begun to worry about the slow, yet seemingly steady decline in the ongoing spiritual experience of the churches. There seemed to be a dip in attendance at the prayer meeting, and while the preaching festivals were still popular they were becoming more festive and less message-orientated. The popular, bardic preachers of the day seemed more concerned about presentation than that which was being presented. The message, still largely orthodox, was clothed in poetic alliteration and 'canned enthusiasm', something that most definitely still entertained and kept the crowds, yet often failed to stimulate spiritual growth and enthusiasm in the hearers. Although this was by no means true of all, it was characteristic of many. The radical, evangelical message of Welsh nonconformity was in danger of becoming the new conformity, slowly solidifying into something more institutional and traditional than its roots might have suggested.

Realising this, many began to long for a return to a more spiritual religion. They felt that the answer was yet another revival, and began to yearn for a visitation that would redress the balance. The Revd George Jones of Llaneurgain, writing in 1902 in a Calvinistic Methodist monthly magazine on the need for religious revival, urges the people of God to pray for it.

> If we are to have another revival in Wales we must rouse the Church to desire it until that desire gets so strong and fervent that we come to feel that it's not possible to be able to live without it.[1]

He goes on to relish the possibility of a revival at the beginning of the twentieth century.

Similar calls to prayer and memories of past revival were to follow.[2] In 1898 Edward Parry published his *Handbook to the History of Religious Revivals in Wales* (*Llawlyfr ar Hanes y Diwygiadau Crefyddol yng Nghymru, 1898*). The other book on the history of Welsh revivals written by Henry Hughes was published in the midst of the divine fire.[3] Many began to long passionately for another national awakening such as that in 1859, when it was estimated that 100,000 were added to the churches.

This desire for renewal was also expressed in action, the Forward Movement of the Presbyterian Church being a good example. This was the evangelistic arm of the Calvinistic Methodist Church of Wales. By 1900 the movement had proclaimed the message to thousands of unchurched people and had planted 30 church centres of worship, 25 of which were in South Wales with 1,937 attending.[4]

At Llandrindod, in 1903, the first Welsh Keswick Convention was held, a conference that energised existing leaders to a proactive mentality, when it came to reaching the lost. Abandoning passivity, these rejuvenated ministers, later to become key revival figures, sought to bring refreshment to their own congregations in the months previous to the revival itself.

R.B. Jones

Those young men returned to the pulpits altogether changed. A new vision had dawned on their souls; spiritual truths had become articulate to their minds; an unwonted power had come into both life and ministry ... They had entered into the experience which follows the receiving of the Holy Spirit in faith. They were cleansed ... from habits which had long defied their best resolves ... The testimony of each in his own church made a deep impression and caused intense questioning ... Soon in some, at least, of their churches there were signs of a real awakening, and many were converted. Many of their members, the young people especially, were led into full surrender to Christ as king and become bold open air witnesses.[5]

These were among the growing number of believers who felt that action must be taken to remedy the spiritual state of the nation. Dean Howell sums up the concern of many, in an article which appeared in the 1902 December issue of *Y Cyfaill Eglwysig*, just a month before his death. Many regarded it in hindsight as prophetic.

What is Wales' greatest need? Some point to the need of political reform ... A better educated ministry? A better health service and social services, all things which are important. But are any of these the main need of Wales at this time? In my estimation there is a greater need than all these, something that will reach into the soul of a nation, something that will create a greater effect than all of them, something more lasting in its fruit and all-encompassing in its blessing spiritual and temporal. Spiritual revival, not reformation but revival. And I don't mean local missions either; rather I'm speaking about the need for a high tide of the Spirit flooding over the whole country that will touch all classes with the baptism of the Holy Spirit. This surely is Wales' greatest need at this time.

> THE NEED FOR A HIGH TIDE OF THE SPIRIT FLOODING OVER THE WHOLE COUNTRY ... THIS SURELY IS WALES' GREATEST NEED AT THIS TIME.

There has never before been so much preaching, but what of the effects? ... From all directions there are complaints that the ministry has lost its power and its convicting edge ... The preaching is scholarly, interesting and educational but there is little anointing and convicting in it. Consciences are not pricked as in days gone by, and old phrases of long ago—such as conviction, conversion, repentance, adoption, dying to sin, self-loathing, etc—have become alien and meaningless, while the old experiences that came out of these phrases have become fossilised and without life.

> THE SPIRIT OF GOD IS THE ONLY SOURCE OF SPIRITUAL LIFE. THERE IS NO WAY TO PRODUCE OR REVIVE THIS LIFE OTHER THAN BY THE INSTRUMENTALITY OF THE SPIRIT.

And the result? Family worship is quickly disappearing ... The Sunday school is only just holding its own. Congregations in many places are lessening. Keeping the Sabbath has become a matter of debate and the prayer meeting is nearly extinct ... The authority of the Bible and the foundational truths of Christianity are being judged in the court of reason and criticism ... Unshakable belief in the unseen, the miraculous and the supernatural is questioned openly. Temperance is not as prosperous as it used to be, with the curse of drink rearing its head in town and countryside ... The desire for pleasure has totally captivated the age ...

But what is the answer? There is no argument about this. If there is such a thing as truth between the covers of the word of God—here it is. The Spirit of God is the only source of spiritual life. There is no way to produce or revive this life other than by the instrumentality of the Spirit. ' "Not by might and not by power but by my Spirit," says the Lord of Hosts' ... It is man's fault and not God's will that there isn't the same unction and authority in the preaching of the gospel in this generation ...

Reader! Will you do your part in this blessed work? Will you give yourself fully to this cause? Morning, midday and night? Will you do your best jointly to work with others so that you can create circles of intercession? Great is your privilege—great too is your responsibility. 'Oh, that you would rend the heavens and come down ...'

... Take note, if this was to be my last message to my fellow country men throughout the length and breadth of Wales before I am taken to the judgment it would remain thus—the greatest need of my dear nation and country at this time is spiritual revival through a specific outpouring of the Holy Spirit. Heavenly Jubilee, let me see the break of day.[6]

This was the Wales into which Evan Roberts was born.

EVAN ROBERTS' EARLY YEARS

Evan Roberts was born at Island House, Bwlchymynydd, the ninth child of Henry and Hannah Roberts, on 8 June 1878. The house is still there although much changed over the years, and unrecognisable from the picture in Dr Phillips' early biography. Yet thousands of pilgrims, from every part of the globe, having visited Moriah and Pisgah, the churches associated with Evan Roberts' name, go the extra mile and visit his birthplace and home for nearly 27 years. The house is situated just a few hundred yards from the banks of the Loughor River, the scene and stage for Evan's early boyhood and adolescence. The plaque outside commemorating the well-known revivalist is the only clue to Island House's historical significance in the development and spread of twentieth-century Christianity.

^ Pisgah Chapel

v Island House

Loughor (Llwchwr or Casllwchwr in Welsh), is situated about eight miles west of Swansea, and three or four miles east of Llanelli. During the final years of the nineteenth century and the early 1900s, it was a comparatively small town linked to the wider world by the Great Western Railway, which spanned the estuary on a fine bridge a mile or so south of Island House. The town had its public hall, police station and its three chapels—Calvinistic Methodist, Congregationalist and Baptist—plus of course an Anglican parish church, which was situated on a rise next to the ruins of a stone Norman castle. A census of the period numbers the population as 2,064, with the numbers rising to 4,190 when the whole parish was included.[1]

Henry Roberts (born 1844), was a native of Loughor, and worked as a pumpman and collier in the local coalmine. Those who knew him described him as hardworking with plenty of go and energy,[2] excitable, lively and with a fiery temperament.[3] Hannah (born 1849), Evan's mother, was a native of Llanon in Carmarthenshire, and had moved to Loughor in her early teenage years to go 'into service', that is to work as a maid. It was here that she met her husband and they were married on 31 March 1868. Described by some as meek, careful with money and sprightly,[4] she was also known for her kindness and heroic spirit.[5] She bore 14 children—seven sons and seven daughters— eight of whom were alive during the time of the 1904 revival. Sarah, the oldest, lived at home with her parents; Catherine and David had married and moved away; Maria and Bessie had emigrated to the USA, while Evan, Dan and Mary were living at home in Island House.[6]

> **HE WAS ONE OF THE MOST WISE, MOST FAIR OF JUDGMENT, MOST EASY-GOING AND KIND OF ALL THAT I CAME TO KNOW ...**

Evan was educated at the National School in Loughor, which he began attending at the age of four or five years. During this time, he showed a real love of reading and learning, winning a book for coming top in his form. Always well-mannered and obedient, he also loved the usual rough-and-tumble of childhood, often engaging in boxing matches with his younger brother Dan. David R. Grenfel (DR), a childhood friend, who later became a well-known politician, speaks of this period.

Interviewer: Now you two were pretty close in age?

DR: Evan was the older, Dan was closer to my age. Evan was about three years older than me.

I: Were you brought up close to Island House?

DR: Not far away, just a few minutes.

I: So you were well acquainted with Evan Roberts as a young boy?

DR: Very much so.

I: What are your impressions as you look back on Evan Roberts as a boy?

DR: He was one of the most wise, most fair of judgment, most easygoing and kind of all that I came to know as a child.

I: What else would you say about him? Was he a sportsman or an athlete?

DR: Yes, he was clean-living. Tall, attractive, with a great love of play and playing. We used to spend much time down on the marsh, in and out of the water every quarter of an hour, running and playing all sorts of games. We used to have boxing gloves and we would box with one another. Evan with Dan, and me with my brother ... sometimes spending whole afternoons playing.

I: Was he at all religious at this time?

DR: Yes, but the best word to describe him would be 'idealistic'. Not specifically religious, but he was an idealistic and moral young man.

I: With a clean life?

DR: Oh, yes, with a clean life.[7]

Evan Roberts the boxer was a lifesaver as well, twice rescuing his brother Dan—once from drowning and once after Dan had fallen down a well near his home. There is another story of Evan bravely saving Jenkin Evans, a friend who had got himself into serious trouble in one of the nearby streams. Evan rescued him although unable to swim himself at the time.

Evan's childhood came to an abrupt end some months before his twelfth birthday. His father had broken his leg in an accident at the Mountain Colliery, and had been laid off for three months. Limping badly, he needed assistance to carry out his work. Evan left full-time education to assist his father in carrying water and oil from place to place. By the age of 12 he was working as a door-boy in the mine, opening and closing the doors underground, for the trams to pass.

Working men's language was notoriously bad, and Evan's sheltered childhood had not prepared him for the obscenities that he was now hearing, his first instinct being to get out of earshot as soon as possible. Along with bad language, there were bad conditions to match. While working as a door-boy he nearly became a fatality, when one of the trams broke loose and came

Miners at work

close to crushing him to death. The first pay he received at the colliery—five shillings a week—was small, yet to Evan this meant he was no longer a boy but a working man and proud of it.

As time went on, he was given greater responsibility in the mine, and by his sixteenth year he took on the responsibility of working a heading, earning five shillings a day. When working at the Mountain Pit, aged 16, Evan travelled to Blaengarw to seek employment. After a stay of six weeks, work was again found for him at Loughor in the Broad Oak Mine, where he worked until September 1902, with a break of a few weeks at Mountain Ash (August to September 1899). By then, he was earning better money and, due to his honest and trustworthy character, had become a union man representing his workmates with management. Never afraid of a challenge, he was often involved, during this time, as one of the mines' rescue team. Rescue was to remain a high priority throughout his life.

EVAN'S SPIRITUAL GROWTH

Evan's early spiritual development, at Moriah Calvinistic Methodist Chapel, was typical of the period. Regularly attended, with its plethora of meetings for singing, preaching, prayer and discussion, the chapel became the centre of his social, educational and spiritual life.

Evan's conversion there can be dated to some time prior to his thirteenth birthday. This was no sudden dramatic conversion, but growing evidence of a young boy wholly set on seeking God, something that was seen to develop over the next years. Challenged one night by a question posed by an elder in a meeting, 'What if the Spirit descended and you were absent?', Evan immediately began to pray for a greater and deeper experience of the Spirit. As he noted some years later,

> **EVAN IMMEDIATELY BEGAN TO PRAY FOR A GREATER AND DEEPER EXPERIENCE OF THE SPIRIT.**

> I said then to myself—I will have the Spirit. And through all weather, and in spite of all difficulties, I went to the meetings. Many times, on seeing other boys with the boats on the tide, I was tempted to turn back and join them. But, no. Then I said to myself: Remember your resolve to be faithful and on I went. Prayer meeting Monday evening at the chapel; prayer meeting Tuesday evening at Pisgah (Sunday school branch); church meeting Wednesday evening; Band of Hope Thursday; class Friday evening—to these I went faithfully throughout the years.[1]

And it wasn't only attendance; for Evan Roberts it was active involvement. When in 1893 the Sunday school was opened in the colliery offices near Evan's home, he soon became a teacher and a secretary, later taking on the job of superintendent. He continued his active involvement when a more permanent building was erected for this purpose in 1895, even involving himself with the erection of an iron fence to guard the sanctuary. The chapel for him was a cause to be supported at all costs, and no task was too small for him to undertake. Just before leaving for Newcastle Emlyn in September 1904, he was even been in charge of the pew rents. (It was still the custom in many chapels to pay for the family seat.) This job he then passed on to his brother. Interestingly, payments detailed in a later rent book show the family pew of Island House to be number 45, literally the back row (Pew Rent Book, Moriah Chapel).

Evan praying

The Bible was a familiar book to Evan throughout his adolescence; it was book that seemed to never leave his side. He loved to begin discussion on it at home, and kept a copy at work to read whenever he was able. When in 1895 an explosion in the pit caused his Bible to be damaged and scorched, he wrote up the story in a national children's magazine. He noted that after the explosion (he was not on shift), he went searching for the remains of his well-read copy. Seeing symbolism even in the search, he wrote, 'I had to go to seek the truth on my knees.'

Later, during the revival, he would show this copy to friends and journalists, giving pages of it as mementoes. It is now kept at the National Library of Wales. A contemporary workmate remembers how, as his workmates passed him on the way into the mine, the young Evan would share Bible verses with them, asking them to think over the passage before they passed him on the way out.

He was as dedicated to prayer, public and private. He not only attended the prayer meeting but, having overcome some initial fear of being asked to pray by the minister, he also regularly took part publicly, taking great care in the use of his vocabulary as he did so.[2]

His passion for public prayer prompted him to encourage others in the practice, and he held classes for boys with this specifically in mind, even writing prayers for those who felt a little too nervous to compose their own. Some of these meetings were not led in the usual way, with the minister asking certain people to lead in prayer, but left open to the promptings of the Spirit,[3] which was something that was to become the norm in Evan's revival services.

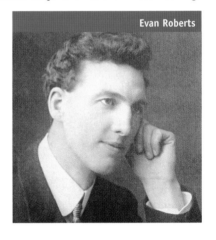
Evan Roberts

The spiritual and religious atmosphere of the Roberts' home was obviously a powerful influence on Evan's life. As in many homes of the time, religion was taken seriously and chapel attendance was regular. Yet from early on, Evan's spiritual growth takes on a more independent and individual course. His commitment to the 'means of grace' was personal and enthusiastic, and it wasn't long before his piety was regarded as being beyond the average. Evan was seen as the spiritually minded one of them by other family members. He was given a room to be left alone in, and he was not to be disturbed. He was the regular initiator of conversation centred around the Bible and the faith, other family members responding to him. It is interesting to note that during these years Island House had no family altar (that is, set family worship consisting of Scripture reading and prayer). This began only in the first week of November 1904. The Roberts' Christianity was individualistic and private, while Evan's commitment tended to be more in the open and fervent.

This spiritual dedication underlines the extraordinariness of Evan Roberts' Christian walk. Although often described as an ordinary coalminer, it would be untrue to say that he was just an ordinary Christian. His dedication and commitment to God throughout his youth and early manhood was clearly far above the norm, 'above and beyond the call of religious duty', something that was noticed by family, workmates, friends and fellow-churchgoers alike. Evan's future usefulness during the months of revival can never be divorced

Pilgrim's Progress

from those years of extraordinary spiritual development, previous to the powerful and mystical experiences of the Spring of 1904 and at Blaenannerch.

And there were other influences, for example his books. His theological library, while not extensive, was large for a working man at the beginning of the twentieth century. His reference works included the classics of nineteenth-century Welsh spirituality and theology, including the *Welsh Bible Dictionary* of Thomas Charles, a treasury of biblical and theological thought. And there was *Outlines of Theology* by A.A. Hodge, a strongly Calvinistic exposition of Christian truth, also Alexander Cruden's *Concordance of the Holy Scriptures* and Ellicott's *Bible Commentary*. Other books that influenced him were the *Hyfforddwr*, a catechism of Calvinistic theology used by his denomination; John Bunyan's *The Pilgrim's Progress*, a household work in Welsh translation throughout nineteenth-century Wales; and the Calvinistic *Methodist*

Hymnbook, full of poetic expressions of the felt truth of Welsh evangelical Christianity.[4]

Besides these, the religious novels of Sheldon were influential, *In His Steps or What Would Jesus Do*, including numerous books detailing the history of religious revival. He himself noted, 'I could sit up all night to read or talk about revivals.' Yet his reading was wide enough not to exclude good novels and various works of poetry. His delight in Christianity hadn't alienated him from his cultural and national roots. He loved poetry and sought to express himself throughout his life in poetic verse, confessing to a friend in 1899, 'I can assure you that nothing gives me as much pleasure as writing a few poems'.[5]

Evan continued to write poetry in Welsh and in English throughout his life, expressing the heights and depths of his spiritual and emotional life and letting those to whom he showed them in some way into his inner world.

THE FORGE

Evan Roberts' 12-year period as a coalminer came to an end in the late summer of 1902 when he lost his employment, due to a strike at the mine. This was an opportunity for a new beginning, and on 15 September 1902 he went to work as an apprentice blacksmith with his uncle Evan Edwards at Forest, Pontardulais, some four miles or so from his home. The learning of a trade might enable him eventually to travel to America from where, having made money to retire on, he would return again to Wales. Thomas Francis, an early biographer and family friend, notes that even at this early stage Evan had the idea of a self-supporting ministry, with his trade becoming a 'tent-making' job, which would enable him to be involved in missionary work. The idea of being paid to preach was always alien to his personality.

EVAN HAD THE IDEA OF A SELF-SUPPORTING MINISTRY ... THE IDEA OF BEING PAID TO PREACH WAS ALWAYS ALIEN TO HIS PERSONALITY.

Beginning an apprenticeship at 24 was unusual, and Evan had to work and concentrate hard as he began to learn new skills. Instead of the coalface it was understanding the fire, bellows and anvil, along with getting to grips with shoeing horses—one of the most difficult jobs that the apprentice blacksmith had to learn. Work at the forge also included long 12-hour shifts—eight in the morning to eight at night—on weekdays, as well as Saturday mornings; a factor that curtailed his usual involvement with the mid-week meetings at Libanus Chapel, Pontardulais.

During his time at Pontardulais he seemed to please his uncle with the progress he was making at his trade. According to Edwards, Evan 'was an excellent worker. There was only one other who was able to shoe horses as quick and often quicker than him but there was nothing but shoeing horses on his mind'.[1] And there was more than the work of a blacksmith on Evan's mind at this time. Although unable to attend as many meetings as he did at Moriah and Pisgah his continued devotion to all things spiritual again became evident to those with whom he lodged and came into contact. The Bible continued to be his delight. As when he was in the coalmine, it never seemed to be far from his side, whether he was working at the forge or sitting by the fireside at his lodgings next door. He had already read the Bible through from cover to cover, three times, twice in Welsh and once in English, and continued to study it on every possible occasion, including meal times.

The Welsh Bible

Y BIBL CYSEGR-LAN

EVAN ... RESOLVED WITH UNFLINCHING DETERMINATION TO DEVOTE HIS WHOLE LIFE TO JESUS CHRIST AND HIS WORK.

Generally regarded as a quiet person at this time, happy with his own thoughts and company, Evan would come to life when religious subjects were discussed, gladly making his own contribution. His maternal grandmother, Sara Edwards, who also lived next to the forge during his apprenticeship, spoke of the ongoing fellowship she had with her grandson as he read and prayed with her during his stay. She spoke too of the regular discussions as to the correct mode of baptism. She was a thorough-going Baptist; Evan of course was a Calvinistic Methodist and held to infant baptism. Although 92 years of age, she was reported to have the better of him at least in this argument.

During the working day, Evan seemed continually taken up with spiritual themes, showing pastoral concern even for his fellow worker at the forge as he sought to help him to pray publicly by writing out prayers. He was also known for his occasional rendering of a Welsh hymn while at work. According to Thomas Francis it was during this time that Evan composed some of his best poetry and, when possible, he competed at literary meetings held at local chapels, often taking the accolade.

Yet there was a growing unease in his soul throughout 1903.

> I used to be ashamed of myself at the thought that everybody was working with some object to aim at while I had none. This made me restless and unsatisfied with everything that I undertook.[2]

D.M. Phillips continues the story:

> One Friday night, when following this new occupation, he had been sending home a friend of his, Mr W.H. Morgan, who was a student in the ministry. On his way back, Evan Roberts resolved with unflinching determination to devote his whole life to Jesus Christ and his work. 'From that time on,' said he, in relating the account, 'my mind was in a perpetual state of commotion with the desire to entirely devote myself to work for Jesus.'[3]

Later he was to confess in an interview with the Llanelli paper that, deep down, entering the ministry was something that had always been on his mind, his secular work always taking second place.[4] The possibility of going into full-time ministry had been suggested to him for years by a number of his acquaintances, his schoolteacher, his co-worker at the Sunday school, and his minister. His father had once even offered to pay the expenses for his training, but until now it hadn't been the right time.[5]

Having made this decision, Evan now saw his apprenticeship at the forge as a hindrance to God's calling on his life. While working at the bellows in the forge he was heard to say, 'Men speak of white slaves; here is a white slave, I in this place'.[6] The ongoing struggle came to a climax on 17 December 1903, when he decided to leave his apprenticeship and to apply for training for Christian ministry. A letter written to a friend a month earlier gives us insight into his mind and motive at the time.

Forest, Llanedi
Pontardulais
18 November 1903

Respected brother,

I know you will be surprised when you understand the message of this note, and I am surprised myself, and without any more ado, the message is this: I have determined to give up my vocation, and join the same calling as you.

Will you believe this? I have had quite enough of bodily labour as my soul thirsts for knowledge and a wider sphere of usefulness.

I know I am going on in age, but am I too old? There was a time in my life when the desire was strong, but when I understood that the influence of the 'schools' destroyed the spirit of the ministerial students I had no heart within me anymore to venture there. But now I see no other means whereby I may ascend the pulpit and like all the others, I am resolved to tread the same path. But to tell you the truth, I am often on the verge of weeping at my ignorance, and I nearly 26 years old. Oh! What a gulf between us! But if this is the Lord's will 'may it be done' hard though it be.

Remember, I have not mentioned a word to 'Jones' nor any of the church. I have informed them at home, and it is surprising how glad they are! But is there ground for gladness?

Will you be good enough to send me your **opinion (not your feeling)** *and your advice? Thanks, if you will. It will be reasonable for you to ask what is the cause for this. Well, to tell you candidly, I have been with Professor Williams, phrenologist, Swansea and this is what he said: 'That I would a. succeed and b. excel in electricity etc, but seeing how strong were my moral and religious capacities, that I could and ought to think seriously of the Pulpit and that it was folly for me to have ever taken to bodily labour ...*

On searching, I find the following things urge me to this:

1. A passionate desire of my soul for ten years, which I could not destroy. If the desire came when I was sad and low only, I would think nothing of the pulpit, but when on the heights of joy and success and whenever I heard a sermon whether good or poor, this was the cry, 'The pulpit for me'.

2. The voice of the people. You may not know anything concerning this. While on a visit to Builth I went to a prayer meeting and took part. After the service was over, the minister asked me if I were a student. I answered, 'No'. Then he advised me, 'Look here, young man, you have talents for the pulpit. Do not abuse them. It is a matter for prayer. Yes, my friend pray over it, pray over it.' Others from the church at Moriah and Mountain Ash together with Jones Mountain Ash.

3. The infinite love of God and his promise of the Holy Spirit. Last Sunday evening as I was meditating on the greatness of the work and my danger in dishonouring the glory of the Lord I could not refrain from weeping. And I prayed that the Lord would baptise you and me with the Holy Spirit. I have no sermon ready. I wonder will I be received by the church at Moriah, and the district after that.

I am, humbly, and wishing you success and God-speed
E.J. Roberts c/o Evan Roberts[7]

On Sunday evening 18 December 1903, Evan Roberts preached his first sermon at his home church of Moriah, Loughor. He preached on Luke 9:23: 'Then he said to them all: "If anyone would come after me, he must deny himself and take up his cross daily and follow me."'

From December 1903 to September 1904, Evan Roberts spent his time at home in Island House preparing himself for entry into the Calvinistic Methodist ministry. This was a time of sitting exams and preaching some sermons in the local chapels. It was during this time that he became friendly with Sydney Evans, who was to become a key figure later, in the revival. He too was preparing to enter the grammar school and apply for the Christian ministry. He was later to marry Evan Roberts' sister Mary. During the Spring of 1904, Evan began to experience an ongoing and intense encounter with God. He tells the story himself.

'Taken up'—Spring 1904

For a long time I was much troubled in my soul and my heart by thinking over the failure of Christianity—oh! It seemed such a failure—such a failure and I prayed and prayed, but nothing seemed to give me any relief. But one Friday night last spring *after I had been in great distress praying about this,* I was taken up to a great expanse—without time and space. It was communion with God. *I found myself with unspeakable joy and awe in the very presence of the almighty God. I was privileged to speak face to face with him as a man speaks face to face with a friend.* Before this, a far-off God I had. I was frightened that night, but never since. So great was my shivering that I rocked the bed, and my brother, being awakened, took hold of me thinking I was ill.

After that experience I was awakened every night a little after one o'clock. This was strange, for through the years I slept like a rock, and no disturbance in my room would awaken me. From that hour I was taken up into the divine fellowship for about four hours. What it was I cannot tell you, except that it was divine.

> **I SAW THINGS IN A DIFFERENT LIGHT AND I KNEW THAT GOD WAS GOING TO WORK IN THE LAND, AND ... IN ALL THE WORLD.**

I felt it and it seemed to change all my nature and I saw things in a different light and I knew that God was going to work in the land, and not this land only but in all the world. About five o'clock I was again allowed to sleep on till about nine.

At this time I was again taken up into the same experience as in the early hours of the morning until about twelve or one o'clock. They questioned me at home, why didn't I get up earlier etc, etc. But it was too divine to say anything about it. This went on for about three months. When I went to school, to Newcastle Emlyn— oh! I was afraid that I would lose the communion. I had set aside half an hour daily for it. And for the first week I did the school work very well. But after that all the time was taken up ...[8]

Revival at New Quay in West Wales

At the time that Evan Roberts was experiencing his 'face-to-face' encounter with God in the Spring of 1904, God's Spirit was also at work among a group of young people at Tabernacle Church, New Quay.

The minister, Joseph Jenkins, had been concerned about the spiritual life of the church in his area for some time and had already held a 'Convention for the Deepening of the Spiritual Life' at New Quay, 31 December 1903–1 January 1904, the speakers being Mr and Mrs J.M. Saunders and W.W. Lewis. This had been seen as a success.[9] Other conferences had been planned: the second in Aberaeron 30 June–1 July and the third at Blaenannerch in September 1904.[10]

Jenkins himself seemed to be going through a personal spiritual reformation around the time. He had met with his nephew regularly—John Thickens, a minister at Aberaeron—to discuss their own spiritual state—meetings that to begin with only highlighted their own spiritual need. But a deeper realisation of spiritual truth began to dawn on Jenkins after he read Andrew Murray's *With Christ in the School of Prayer* and a biography of US evangelist Dwight L. Moody.[11]

This led to nights spent in prayer and at least one intense spiritual experience that he described to a friend years later.[12] One night he was on his knees praying and, having lost all sense of time, he decided to lay hold on God until he was clothed with power from on high. It was on this night also that he experienced what he described as a 'blue flame', which enshrouded him, and which he took as a sign of the intense spiritual communion that he had experienced.

This 'communion' was soon to affect his own congregation. About February 1904 Jenkins was preaching on 1 John 5:4: 'for everyone born of God overcomes the world. This is the victory that has overcome the world, even our faith.' After the service he was approached by a young girl who said that she longed for spiritual peace and joy. Jenkins advised her that she should acknowledge the *Lordship* of Christ over her life and submit to the leading of the Holy Spirit. One Sunday in February 1904 in the youth meeting, she stood up and publicly confessed that she loved the Lord Jesus with all her heart.

The effect was electrifying and deep beyond description—gentle weeping spread through the congregation. After this the numbers of young people in attendance grew week by week. Some travelled up to 15 miles to attend the weekly youth meetings.[13] The zeal of the youth grew and many of them, accompanied by their minister, soon began spreading the fire to other chapels in West Wales.

A recently found letter, written in the spring of 1904 from New Quay to the Revd J.T. Job, highlights the spiritual intensity experienced by the youth of Jenkins' church. This letter leaves little doubt that what was being experienced at New Quay was not just a precursor to revival but revival itself.

Letter from his father-in-law to J.T. Job

8 Marine Terrace
New Quay
5 May 1904

Dear son-in-law,

I have been thinking for days and weeks of writing you a letter (to break this quietness), to give you the history of the revival here amidst the young people more specifically. Yet the gentle atmosphere is also on the middle-aged and the old. They are being called 'Christian Endeavour Meetings'. In the end many of these meetings break out in praise to God ... Some praying while others halfway through the prayers break out to sing, young girls mainly, girls in service going forward to pray without being asked.

There is a meeting after the morning sermon in the vestry. All these meetings are held in the vestry with the preachers going into them and some of the preachers experiencing emotions that they never had ever before. The eyes of all are filled with tears when the girls pray. (I will name some of them:) Florrie Evans is about 20 years of age, she lives a few doors above us in this street. She is about the first that the Spirit came upon. Maude Davies (the singer); May Phillips of Park Street; Maggie Davies (a maid who is with Mrs Phillips); Dd. [Dafydd] Jenkin Evans Wellington (he was in the church but he has come to us now), and he is full of the Holy Spirit as in the days of the apostles. And there are a number of girls that take part ... reading a psalm, giving out a word to sing, and tens of others. There is a meeting every Wednesday evening and they come here three or four miles distance from the county. The place was last night over-packed (old drunkards are coming in, and in the meeting they shout out for prayer and are praising God before they come out). Yes, this is how it is now. I hope this is how it will continue. It is easy to pray and preach here ...

(letter courtesy of Revd Dafydd Job)

Ministers visiting the area noticed the change. According to the Revd R.B. Jones who visited New Quay in August, 'the fire was burning'.[14] Seth Joshua, who was conducting a mission there in September, records in his diary:

There is a remarkable revival spirit here. I have never seen the power of the Holy Spirit so powerfully manifested among the people as at this place just now. The revival is breaking out here in greater power—the young are receiving the greatest measure of blessing. They break out into prayer, praise, testimony and exhalation in a wonderful way. Several souls.[15]

Joseph Jenkins himself describes the outpouring in a letter to Evan Philips in March.

28 March 1904

The Spirit of God has fallen on our young people. I am unable to do anything. I am in the middle of the sound of the **wind.** *God himself is here. I have never seen anything like it before. It is Spring and I don't know what to say—only weep and yet I cannot weep. Twenty-year-old girls are prophesying. It is the early hours of the morning and I am unable to go to bed. I must try to pray. I know that you will be pleased to hear this news. I do not know where to start with anything. I organised a meeting for the youth before and ... the tide now is truly powerful.*

Yours Jos Jenkins[16]

When Evan Roberts arrived at Newcastle Emlyn in September 1904, he was to come to an area where people were already *burning* with spiritual enthusiasm.

Apart from works already cited, the general information for the period covered in this chapter is contained in Tudor Rees, 'Evan Roberts' life and work', *Sunday Companion*, 11 February 1905, p.644; Robert Ellis, *Living Echoes of the Welsh Revival 1904–1905*, London, Delyn Press, pp.22-23; and B.p.Jones, *An Instrument of Revival: The Complete Life of Evan Roberts 1878–1951*, South Plainfield, NJ, Bridge Publishing, p.13.

Grammar School, Newcastle Emlyn

NEWCASTLE EMLYN
INSIGHT – HISTORY: GRAMMAR SCHOOL

The grammar school at Newcastle Emlyn was popular with students for the ministry. They came here to prepare themselves for the ministerial college at Trefecca. At the beginning of the century there would have been 30 or 40 students present, most of whom had already learnt a trade, some as coalminers, farm workers or carpenters. The headmaster at the time was John Phillips, son of the Revd Evan Phillips. He was highly regarded by the students. Determined to get them into ministerial college, he would often spend extra time with those who needed added tuition and many appreciated his efforts. During Evan Roberts' short stay at the school, from 13 September to 31 October 1904, he was remembered as a quiet boy of good character with something pleasant and likeable in his personality. He lodged just a few hundred yards from the grammar school at Ty-Llwyd with his close friend, Sydney Evans. Between Ty-Llwyd and the school was Sunnyside, the home of Evan Phillips.

D.J. Evans, a fellow student, adds that Evan was conscientious in his work. This might have been the case for the first week and a half, but Evan was ill and bedridden from 23 to 26 September and, following his experience at Blaenannerch on 29 September, found it increasingly hard even to pick up a textbook, so his time of actual study at the school was minimal. October became a month of spiritual searching for Evan Roberts, according to his friend Sydney, a time of waiting to see what God's guidance was.[1] It also became a time of prayer and fellowship with the New Quay youth, thus leaving precious little time and energy for other, intellectual pursuits. His plans of study and entering the ministry were quickly overtaken by the events of the first few weeks of his stay at the school.[2]

September 1904

Tuesday 13	Enter Newcastle Emlyn Grammar School. Visit Evan Phillips
Sunday 18	Preaching at Twrgwyn in the evening
Friday 23	Absent from school—confined to bed
Saturday 24	Confined to bed
Sunday 25	Confined to bed
Monday 26	Confined to bed
Tuesday 27	Confined to bed
Wednesday 28	First day of Blaenannerch Conference
Thursday 29	The Blaenannerch Experience
Friday 30	Plan to evangelise Wales

October 1904

Saturday 1	Visit New Quay to discuss mission
Thursday 6	Revival meeting at Twrgwyn (preacher: Joseph Jenkins)
Sunday 9	Preaching at Tanygroes, Cardiganshire
Sunday 16	Preaching at Penffordd and Gwastad
Tuesday 18	Bwlchygroes (Pembrokeshire) monthly meeting
Wednesday 19	Bwlchygroes
Friday 28	Revival meeting at Capel Drindod
Saturday 29	Students prayer meeting
Sunday 30	Bethel, Newcastle Emlyn
Monday 31	10.45am train to Loughor

Newcastle Emlyn
13 September—31 October 1904

I had to go to Newcastle Emlyn to the college to prepare for the ministry. I dreaded to go, for fear I should lose the four hours with God every morning. I determined to give it half-an-hour every day, and the remainder to the schoolwork. But I had to go, and it happened as I feared. [For a whole month] ... He came no more, and I was in darkness.

And my heart became as a stone.
Even the sight of the cross brought
no tears to my eyes.[3]

MR. EVAN ROBERTS.

EVAN PHILLIPS, 1829–1912
INSIGHT—BIOGRAPHY

Evan Phillips had been the minister of Bethel Calvinistic Methodist Church at Newcastle Emlyn since 1860 and was a well-known preacher in his denomination. He was no stranger to revival either. During the 1859 revival he had travelled and preached throughout Wales with Dafydd Morgan, a central figure of that awakening, and he would often repeat one of the last things that Dafydd Morgan told him: 'It has gone cold, but it will come again; you will live to see another revival, although I will not'.[4]

Besides living in the atmosphere of revival, Phillips had also experienced the mystical side in a vision he saw at the time, indicating the coming of the revival to a certain Welsh valley and the vision being quickly fulfilled.[5] Here was a man who could understand at least some of what was going on in Evan Roberts' development and sought to provide guidance and balance. Evan went to Mr Phillips with the story of a diabolic face that had mocked him in the garden at the back of his lodgings. 'Maybe it's the fruit of your imagination,' suggested the old, godly philosopher. Evan Roberts insisted that it wasn't subjective. Mr Phillips encouraged him to get down to his books!

Evan Phillips' home, Sunnyside, was just a few yards away from the grammar school that Evan Roberts attended and it became a regular place of fellowship for the students—a home from home. J.H. Howard, a student in the late 1890s, some five years before Evan Roberts, describes the atmosphere:

> The chief attraction for students was the veteran preacher Evan Phillips, father of our principal. His home was an open house for us all. We entered without knocking, and helped ourselves to the tobacco jar always to be found on the table: and then we sat in a circle about the sage who would argue, scold

and bless us according to the prevailing mood or need. If a boy was in the throes of composing a new sermon, our old theologian would give him points, and perhaps preach them himself on the following Sunday.

He summarised books for us, taught us to breathe aright, how to stand before an audience, to produce and regulate the voice, and then brought us face to face with eternal truths. Evan Phillips left his stamp upon generations of students, and was revered throughout Wales. His sermon seldom lasted longer than 20 minutes, but not a word was wasted and each sentence carried weight. I always found him fresh and impressive.[6]

Evan Phillips was his own man—natural, humorous—a character! And with an above-average interest in train-spotting.[7] While not a great reader[8] —he tended to limit his reading to the Bible and the newspaper—he could read people and situations and his godly, down-to-earth advice and example proved precious to many.

Evan Roberts was one of them. Speaking to J.J. Morgan in 1930, Evan Roberts himself describes him:

In his prayers you felt the challenge in his voice. Nothing could stop him. He embraced God.[9] He was a heavenly minded man. He produced a God-atmosphere in his meetings. He was fond of the Lord Jesus Christ. He had natural gifts but God made them great. The purity of the law was seen in his preaching.[10]

Speaking of his impressions of Evan Roberts, Evan Phillips noted: 'Evan Roberts was like a piece of radium in our midst'.[11]

And it wasn't only the father who was to be a witness to Evan Roberts' spiritual journey at Newcastle Emlyn. Evan Phillips' family too were to see and seek to understand the young student from Loughor! His daughters especially were to be witnesses and even players in the spiritual drama that was unfolding in the life of Evan Roberts, and it is evident from their testimony how highly they thought of him. This feeling was shared by Evan Phillips himself who years later spoke warmly and positively about Evan's time at Newcastle Emlyn. Evan Roberts and his team revisited the Sunnyside household in March 1905, just before the Liverpool mission.

As in 1859, the 1904 revival made a profound impression on the bearded patriarch—he had been aware of the refreshing at New Quay since March 1904, informed by Joseph Jenkins;[12] and later testified that 'I didn't weep much in the revival of '59 but I have wept now until I'm soft. In the midst of the greatest tears I've felt the greatest joy'![13]

He was even convicted about his smoking and gave it up for a short time, returning to it for 'medical reasons' later.[14]

First week of September 1904

Have started with (1) Latin; (2) Greek; (3) History; (4) Welsh Grammar; (5) English Grammar; (6) Mathematics.

We have Latin and Greek every morning and History twice a week. We have gone through four reigns—Henry VII; Henry VIII; Edward VI; Mary and next time 'Good Queen Bess'. I have bought Gill's *History of England*. It is so concise, and it is also the book used in the class.

Welsh: we have this subject twice a week
English Grammar: every morning
Mathematics: in the afternoon

Hours—Morning 9.30am—12.00pm
Afternoon 1.30pm—4.00pm[15]

Sydney Evans preached at Solfach last Sunday, about 40 miles from here. I have been preaching also one Sunday evening since I am here at Twrgwyn. We have very kind folk at our lodgings. We pay 3s 6d for lodgings, washing and potatoes included. They also give freely of their own substance. It is a very clean place.[16]

SETH JOSHUA
INSIGHT—BIOGRAPHY

Seth Joshua was an evangelist for the Forward Movement of the Presbyterian Church of Wales. He left Memorial Hall, Cardiff in January 1904,[17] and conducted evangelistic tours throughout that year in England and Wales. His diary records a successful year,[18] with many coming to faith.

Seth had been concerned about revival for a number of years. An entry on 18 November 1904, when the revival had already started, illustrates this:

> This path alongside the River Taff has become sacred to me. I have seen the hawthorn blossom three years in succession and fade again as I have prayed along its shady path. I have wrestled for personal baptism of the Spirit and for a national revival. It has come and I rejoice.[19]

Alongside many other leaders and preachers, Seth had been encouraged by attending the new Llandrindod Conferences of August 1903 and 1904 with their emphasis on full consecration, although he did have some reservations, fearing that holiness might become a substitute for practical service in Christ's cause.[20]

During the summer, autumn and winter of 1904 Seth seems to be at the right place at the right time. In mid-September he conducts a mission in New Quay, followed by another in Newcastle Emlyn (25–30 September). He even catches the wrong train and ends up in Newcastle Emlyn on Friday 16 September, where he uses the time to have tea with Evan Phillips.

On Thursday 29 September, he travels with Evan Roberts in the cart from Newcastle Emlyn to Blaenannerch. Just three hours or so before Evan Roberts' 'baptism' experience, Seth Joshua feels constrained to divulge the fact that he has been praying that God would take a lad from the coalmine or from the field, even as he took Elijah from the plough, to revive His work—someone not from the universities and colleges, which would feed pride and intellectualism. He hasn't mentioned this prayer, which he had prayed for four years, to anyone *until that morning*.[21]

In under three hours it would begin to be answered.

Later Seth's missions at Ammanford and Gorseinon were to coincide with great power and blessing as the revival took off publicly.

Saturday 24 September 1904
Diary of Seth Joshua

I did not get to bed until two o'clock and was up at six to go with the carriage to go to Newcastle Emlyn. What shall I find there? Lord, come with me for I hear Thou art kept outside the door in that town as at Loadicea.[22]

Sunday 25 September 1904

I have tried to give them an account of the revival at New Quay when in the pulpit this morning, but I broke down under the emotion resting on my spirit. Many others wept in the chapel, and there were signs here of a deep desire. I preached four times this day. Nothing has moved yet.[23] (Seth Joshua's diary)

Monday 26 September 1904

There was a touch of power in the service tonight and a few moved toward the cross. I find scarcely a soul here in the joy of assurance. It is a pitiable sight to me. When I tested the meeting only a small handful among hundreds could stand up to confess a present salvation. The witness of a church is nothing in this state. Some souls [were saved].[24] (Seth Joshua's diary)

Compelled to give most of my time to the divine communion ... Confined to my bed by a severe cold for four days ... Prayed day and night, the last of these nights the perspiration poured down my cheeks. This was caused by the cold and my communion with God.[25]

Some of the students came with Sydney Evans to see if I would come to the service. The minute they asked, I felt the Spirit descending on me. The irresistible possessed me, and I rushed to chapel without my overcoat. The divine influence began to bear on me heavily. I was ready to pray—to pray for the girls of New Quay to have strength in the face of the expectations of the people from them. I had been praying Monday evening in the house for strength for them; but the Spirit would not allow me to pray in chapel tonight. It was wonderful on me. I was asking—where is the devil? I felt awfully hard. I looked at the cross without feeling anything. I wept bitterly because of my hardness of heart; but I did not weep because of Christ. I loved the Father and the Holy Spirit, but did not love the Son.[26]

Tuesday 27 September 1904
Diary of Seth Joshua

A large number were blessed this evening. Some students received blessing and confessed salvation. The name of one was Sydney Evans. The Lord will certainly move this place. The yearning is here among the people. Several souls.[27]

JOHN PHILLIPS' TESTIMONY
INSIGHT—WITNESS

Mr John Phillips, his master at the school, relates one very strange petition of [Evan Roberts] at Bethel Chapel, Newcastle Emlyn, when the Revd Seth Joshua was there. Mr Joshua asked if there were any in the meeting who could stand up and sing with him 'O happy day!'. Evan Roberts was one of a few who stood up. On the following night [Wednesday 28 September 1904] Mr Joshua invited people to confess Christ and bend to Him, and Evan Roberts went onto the seat next to the big pew, and prayed with extraordinary intensity. He sent his supplications up to heaven while on his knees with such yearning of spirit and agony of soul that Mr Phillips had never heard the like of it. His tutor then understood that something extraordinary had taken hold of him. He was convinced that Evan Roberts' 'Oh' could not be but the outpouring of a soul in great distress. It came from the depths of his spirit with such feeling as to melt one as he heard it.[28]

Wednesday 28 September 1904, Newcastle Emlyn

Before going to Blaenannerch, I felt like a flint, and told that to Mr Williams the guard, whom I met in Miss Phillips' shop. I felt as if every feeling had been swept from my bosom. I was saying to myself, I must be laid up on a sick bed, or have the Spirit with power. Thanks be to God, I had the Spirit not the sick bed. Miss Magdalen Phillips, the daughter of the Revd Evan Phillips, came to me and asked me to come to their house, to the prayer meeting, which was held before going to Blaenannerch. But I did not go because of two reasons—first, for fear that they would talk about my going out after having been ill for days; second, I wanted to speak to Miss Phillips about her religious condition. I said to her, 'I'll pray for you, you pray for me', and in a moment the tears filled her eyes. Something wonderful happened about 3.30pm, and that I asked Miss Phillips after—'Are you praying for me?' and that she answered, 'Dear Roberts, I was praying for you all day!' [29]

When returning tonight the young women from New Quay tried to influence me, but nothing touched me. And they said: 'We can do nothing for you'? 'No', said I. 'I have only to want for the fire. I have built the altar, and laid the wood in order, and have prepared the offering; I have only to want for the fire'. [30]

SETH JOSHUA
INSIGHT—WITNESS

About 15 young people from New Quay came all the way to Newcastle Emlyn today. I did not preach but allowed them to speak, pray, sing and exhort as the Holy Spirit led them. The fire burned all before it. Souls were melted and many cried out for salvation. Praise the Lord for this service. Many knelt in their seats but I cannot say what the number was. The Master knows. Several souls.[31]

The Chapel at Blaenannerch

W.W. LEWIS, 1856–1938
INSIGHT–BIOGRAPHY

W.W. Lewis was a minister with the Calvinistic Methodists at Seion, Carmarthen. During his time there he had come under the influence of two other ministers in the town—W.S. Jones, the Baptist minister at Penuel and Keri Evans, the Congregational minister at Priory Street, both of whom were spiritually dynamic and were like W.W. to play their part in the coming revival. Their influence, alongside a 'yielding of his entire self to Christ' in a cottage meeting, led to a new grace and meekness in his personality followed by a desire to see others won for Christ.[32]

W.W. [as W.W. Lewis was known] had also been at the first Welsh Keswick Convention for the deepening of the spiritual life at Llandrindod in 1903,[33] and it was this teaching of entire surrender and consecration that he was to bring to the conferences in Cardiganshire. W.W., who had already influenced Joseph Jenkins or John Thickens (it is not stated), was an obvious choice as a speaker. There were five conferences held:

New Quay
Aberaeron
Blaenannerch
Tregarron
New Quay

W.W. was to speak at all of them. He preached on holiness themes such as 'give yourself to God' (Rom. 6:13). He also gave his own testimony publicly.

Jenkins commented that W.W. seemed as if *bathed in the life of Christ*. [34]

During the early months of 1904, W.W.'s hometown of Carmarthen was also to experience the beginnings of a spiritual awakening. At a January mission in the town, a Mr Reader Harries argued that 'Pentecost was still possible for the Church of Christ'. By June, according to the Revd M.H. Jones, minister of the other Calvinistic Methodist church in Carmarthen, heavy showers had fallen on the Sunday morning young people's prayer meeting at Water Street, with girls as well as young men taking part publicly in the meeting.[35] What was happening at Blaenannerch was no new revelation to him.

During the revival itself, W.W. became a key figure in planning conventions for the deepening of the spiritual life of the revival converts. These meetings were to emphasise prayer and practical biblical teaching[36] with the aim of having pure and consecrated churches. Evan Roberts had agreed with this emphasis, noting that if this was the case we would not need to worry about the salvation of the *world*.[37]

Although not unemotional himself, W.W. was wary of emotionalism and sought to give balance to excitable converts who could often see emotion as an end in itself.[38] To a certain brother who had jumped up in excitement and said, 'Isn't it glorious, Mr Lewis?', 'Is it?' responded the minister, 'A calf can jump'.[39] During these times, W.W. proved to be rock of spiritual stability to many ministers who were seeking to know what to do next. The Revd Nantlais Williams of Bethany, Ammanford, called on his help when things seemed to be getting out of control. W.W. responded, 'Keep cool, I'll come'.[40]

29 September 1904

We had 'enthusiastic meetings' at Blaenannerch, but I am afraid the term is too mild. I should say that they were marvellous, because the Holy Spirit was there, working wonderfully. Today's meeting was the most awe-full and pleasant day of my life. The young women of New Quay were there—about 30 in number. And, oh! I should like if such a spirit should fall on the young women of Loughor. Then they would not and could not speak lightly in church, and all their frivolities would be swept away. Some of these young women have been reckless characters. Reading novels; flirting; never reading their Bibles. But now, what a wonderful change. In truth, this is a divine miracle.[41]

We started for Blaenannerch about 6.00am yesterday morning, it lies about eight miles from Newcastle Emlyn. It was a very fine drive through lovely scenery. As we climbed the hills we could see the mist in the valley as if it were a sea. And at one particular place it seemed as if you stood at Pem Beily and looked down towards Penclawdd. The air is very thin here, and it is also so pure, because there are so many hundreds of trees in the neighbourhood, and therefore, it abounds with oxygen.[42]

Now joyful, now sad, now hard and cold—so my feelings varied on the journey. We sang in the break, and my feelings were very varied—now high now low.[43]

The company sang gloriously on their way 'The old time religion' and 'I can prove God answers prayer'.

From Heavenly Jerusalem's towers,
The path through the desert they trace;
And found every affliction they suffered
Redounds to the glory of Grace;
Their look they cast back on the tempests,
On fears, on grim death, and the grave,
Rejoicing that now they're in safety,
Through him that is mighty to save.[44]

The 7.00am meeting was devoted to asking and answering questions. The Revd W.W. Lewis conducted. At the close, the Revd Seth Joshua prayed, and said during his prayer, 'Lord, do this, and this, and this, etc and bend us.' He did not say, 'Oh Lord, bend us.' It was the Spirit that put the emphasis for me on 'bend us'. 'That is what you need', said the Spirit to me. And as I went out I prayed, 'Oh Lord, bend me.'

At the breakfast table at the Revd M.p.Morgan's house, Mag Phillips offered me bread and butter. I refused as I was satisfied. At the same moment the Revd Seth Joshua was putting out his hand to take the bread and butter, and the thought struck me: 'Is it possible that God is offering me the Spirit and that I am unprepared to receive Him; that others are ready to receive but are not offered?' Now my bosom was quite full-tight.

About 9.30am the fire fell and it is burning ever since.[45]

On the way to the 9.00pm meeting, the Revd Seth Joshua remarked, 'We are going to have a wonderful meeting today!' To this I replied, 'I feel myself almost bursting.' The meeting, having been opened, was handed over to the Spirit. I was conscious that I would have to pray. As one and the other prayed

I put the question to the Spirit, 'Shall I pray now?' 'Wait a while,' said He. When others prayed I felt a living force come into my bosom. It held my breath, and my legs shivered and after every prayer I asked, 'Shall I now?' The living force grew and grew, and I was almost bursting. And instantly someone ended his prayer—my bosom boiling. I would have burst if I had not prayed. What boiled me was that verse, 'God commending His Love'. I fell on my knees with my arms over the seat in front of me, and the tears and perspiration flowed freely. I thought blood was gushing forth. Mrs Davies, Mona, New Quay came to wipe my face. On my right was Mag Phillips and on my left Maud[e] Davies. For about two minutes it was fearful. I cried, 'Bend me! Bend me! Bend us!' Then, 'Oh! Oh! Oh! Oh!' and Mrs Davies said, 'Oh wonderful grace!' 'Yes,' I said, 'Oh, wonderful grace!!' What bent me was God commending His love, and I not seeing anything in it to commend. I was bent in body and soul until my face was black and blue. After I was bent a wave of peace came over me. Oh wonderful, this is life! You've heard it said of joy being felt by men to the tops of their fingers. Yes, it is literally true. Oh wonderful, this is a happy life. And the audience sang, 'I hear thy welcome voice!' And as they sang I thought of the bending at the Judgment Day, and I was filled with compassion for those who would be bent on that day. And I wept.[46]

He returned to me, and I had again the glorious communion.[47]

Seth Joshua

I believe the total for this mission is certainly 20 souls. Grand meetings today at Blaenannerch and many cried for mercy. It was a remarkable thing to hear one young man, Evan Roberts. He caught at the words and prayed, 'Bend me, oh Lord.' By some mistake I was obliged to walk back to Newcastle Emlyn and did not reach the chapel till nine thirty; Satan was in this but he did not gain all the victory. The people were still there, having been there since seven o'clock. Wearied as I was, I spoke to them until ten thirty and they listened to my experience. [48]

MAG PHILLIPS OR MAUDE DAVIES
THURSDAY 29 SEPTEMBER 1904
INSIGHT—WITNESS

'I was sitting next to him at this meeting,' said one of the young ladies, 'and I shall never forget the scene. The man was moved in the most extraordinary way and we all felt that something great was happening in his life just then. The Spirit worked within him in all its power and while his whole body quivered with emotion. With only the greatest difficulty could he restrain himself and keep his seat. Then later he rose and in a torrent of new born eloquence he told the astonished gathering how the Holy Spirit for which he had been praying for the last 13 years had now descended on him in all its plenitude of grace.'[49]

Friday 30 September 1904

I was on fire with a desire to go through all Wales, and if it were possible, I was willing to pay God for allowing me to go.[50]

I have received three great blessings: (1) I have lost all nervousness; (2) I can sing all day long—some physical impediment obstructed me before; (3) I had gone as hard as a flint, and that, bear in mind, although my whole inclination and the only object of my life was to serve God—but thank heaven, I was bent low at Blaenannerch. I was so bent that I had to shout out, 'Diolch Iddo!' (Thanks be to Him). Oh! What an easy thing it is to thank now.[51]

Saturday 31 September 1904

My heart was ever like a stone,
My tongue still as the grave;
But from another world there shone
A light my soul to save.

Now, I am singing all day long
The praises of His blood;
No other theme awakes my song
Like Calv'ry's crimson flood.

I felt the pressure of His hand
Bending my sinful heart;
Henceforth, no power can command
My soul from Him to part.[52]

Intended ten to go on mission:

Maud[e] Davies
Elsie Phillips
Mary C. Jones
Miss Davies
Mrs Davies, Mona, New Quay
Florrie Evans
Mrs Evans, New Quay
Sydney Evans
Evan Roberts

Who shall go?
Where shall we go?
When shall we go?

These questions were put on our two small Bibles in the bedroom, in the Lord's presence. For some time we could not enter to see if there was an answer, because we feared entering the room. After having been to Blaenannerch the room had become a holy of holies unto us. Who was to go in first to look at the papers? Both of us [Evan and his fellow student, Sydney Evans] were filled with awe at the thought. However, I had strength to look; but there was nothing on the paper. Immediately the Spirit told me, 'You have not a sufficient number of questions. You should have asked, "Shall we go?"' I saw at once that we had taken the whole thing into our hands, because, 'Shall we go?' should have been the first question.[53]

Thursday 6 October 1904

Some of us have agreed to ask the Lord for 100,000 souls in Wales for Jesus Christ. I have seen Jesus Christ presenting a sort of cheque to His Father on which is written 100,000 and it's all right.[54]

We have come into contact with the young men and young women of New Quay, in this town, at Blaenannerch, and Twrgwyn. We had one awful meeting at Blaenannerch, but we had a wonderfully sweet meeting at Twrgwyn. The service commenced at 6.15pm and closed at 10.15pm. Four hours' meeting, and no one but the young people taking part.[55]

A Saturday in October 1904

After Sydney Evans had gone to bed at 10.00pm, I determined to work at my lessons with all my energy; but suddenly, it came to my mind that I had received some blessing and had not thanked for it. I went to the Throne to thank immediately. After having thanked, I returned to my lessons. But before commencing, I looked what time it was, and said, 'Wonderful! It is 11.00pm.' After that I said, 'Dear me!' And I began thinking how I went to lose an hour's time, and when I looked again another had gone. I jumped at my feet, and hurried to my bedroom in order to have rest. When I entered, Sydney asked, 'What is the time?' 'Twelve,' I said. 'You have had a good time of it?' 'Yes, but not in the Greek.'[56]

Monday 10 October 1904

I am in splendid health—enjoying myself, or rather enjoying heaven greatly.[57]

I have lost all nervousness; I am courageous for Christ, and joyful in Christ. I am healthy and joyful.[58]

There is a blessed time awaiting the Church of Christ in the near future. The night begins to vanish, and the dawn extends gradually but certainly.[59]

The wheels of the gospel chariot are to turn rapidly ere long. And to be permitted to have a hand with the cause is a privilege.[60]

Christ must be glorified. And He will be glorified before long. A great revival is breaking on our country. A blessed time awaits the Christian Church.[61] The night begins to vanish, and the dawn extends gradually but certainly. [62]

Tuesday 11 October 1904

The devil is at his best these days. He attacks me with all his might; and he also ploughs the past of my life. But I rejoice that all has been done away with through the virtue of the blood ... I was having great pleasure with the work before, but now I am having the most pure joy on earth. And, oh! I cannot say how happy I feel, because God works so powerfully on me, and has worked powerfully on me of late. Have come into contact with the young girls of New Quay, and the divine fire has began to lay hold of us. And, oh! it is a blessed time on us, and I wish the fire came to the neighbourhood of Loughor.[63]

Week of 28 October 1904

Regarding the Capel Drindod meeting everything points to a large gathering of young people, and so there will be a splendid place to work for the Great Master. I know that prejudice will be strong against the movement; therefore, we must be armed with the Holy Spirit. Amongst many, too, there will be levity, and this calls upon us to be very watchful with regard to our movements and our words, and remember to keep our eyes from all wantonness. There will be another class, viz., some who come out of curiosity, and possibly some will come to scoff. Therefore, what will be necessary for us to do is to be strong in prayer. Oh! that we could all feel that we can do nothing without the Holy Spirit, and in that feeling fall in lowliness before God with a broken heart, beseeching Him to show us His face, especially at Capel Drindod. It would be awful for us without God.[64]

TESTIMONY OF RACHEL PHILLIPS,
CAPEL DRINDOD, 28 OCTOBER 1904
INSIGHT—WITNESS

'Great was our anxiety that night about Evan Roberts. He was bent on looking heavenwards continually and we, poor creatures, endeavouring to get him to look earthwards.'[65]

Rachel relates to a conversation between herself and Evan Roberts as he turned in to Miss Phillips' shop:

> The morning after the meeting at Capel Drindod, he turned in to me on his way home from the students' prayer meeting, and said that he had a wonderful night. 'I did not sleep all night,' he said. 'The divine outpouring was so heavy that I had to shout out and ask God to withhold his hand.' He failed to rest, and had to get up with the dawn and go out to the hills; and only God and himself know what blessed time he had this morning. After he had finished relating about the night, I told him that I had not experienced the same influence as the others. Then he inquired of me if the Holy Spirit had asked me to do something that I having refused to obey. I said, 'No, I do not think. But I have felt many times on Sundays that I would like to repeat some hymn, were it not that I fear people would think that I want to show myself.' 'Oh, yes,' he remarked; 'That is it, refusing to do a small thing like that is sufficient for him. Obedience must be given in the smallest thing. It looks small to us; but when obeying the blessing comes.'[66]

TESTIMONY OF ANN PHILLIPS, CAPEL DRINDOD, 28 OCTOBER 1904 INSIGHT—WITNESS

I have written concerning Evan Roberts in my own way. If there will be a gem in it (although every word he said is a gem to me), will you take it out and polish it? I shall begin at Capel Drindod. Here Evan Roberts made a deep impression on me. The Revd Joseph Jenkins and the girls from New Quay were there holding a revival meeting. Roberts went up early in the afternoon to prepare himself for the six o'clock service. When I arrived I asked Sydney Evans where Roberts was. He answered that he was in the wood praying. Before long he came to us cheerfully. I was very anxious about him at the time; and they had told me at home to keep my eye on him. After all had gone in, he was out; and it was obvious that something weighed heavily on him. I told him, 'It is better for you to come in; then the burden will fall off.' I knew that it was the meeting that burdened his mind. He commenced his way, but stopped in the lobby. Now I saw his countenance changing and his eyes closed. [His] Looking at me caused me great fear. Then he said, 'Jesus Christ tonight is going to be glorified, more tonight than at Twrgwyn.' I was surprised to hear him saying that. But the reason for my surprise was that I did not understand him. I said to him, 'It is better for you to go in or else we shall not find room.' At the time he wasn't aware if he was in or out of the meeting, because of his absent-mindedness.

After entering he had his eyes closed again, and was under some wonderful influences. The meeting went on excellently in singing and prayer; but before long it began to cool, because speaking took the place of prayer and praise. Consequently we said that to one another. 'Yes, the meeting is going down,' said Roberts, 'and I cannot bear this.' At once he was on his feet and saying fervently that Jesus was not glorified as he should be, because people wanted to show themselves. With these words he fell in the pew, and prayed in such a manner that no one in the audience had ever heard such a prayer. His words burnt the consciences and hearts of many who were present. Soon after he rose from his knees, he asked me to sing.

I asked him not to do so, and said that I would sing with him. But that would not do. I refused about five times; but at last I did and he accompanied me, full of fervour. When near home that night, he called me one side and said, 'Your name is on the book tonight.' I could not understand him. 'Why that?' I said. 'Oh, because thou didst obey,' said he, 'it was written.' Thanks for the meeting in Capel Drindod. It will be with me eternally.[67]

28 October 1904

We have a family altar here at Ty-Llwyd. Sydney leads one night, and I the other, it is a great blessing.[68]

I have not done much with my work since I am here, but I may do so before long. Spiritual things have had such a hold on me, and also on Evans and a young man from Ynyshir—a Mr Jones. But Jones can work like a tiger, and Evans can work very well, but at times he can do nothing. I can see him now at this table writing a letter to some person; it is 10.00am Friday morning. Both of us are not at school this morning. Last night neither of us could work.

How busy the devil is at this place. We have met the young girls from New Quay at Newcastle Emlyn and at Blaenannerch and Twrgwyn. They, the people of this place, make such awful stories, which are downright lies. Some say we go to see the young girls, and not for the cause. Others ask (but not in our faces) how is it that we three and not others have felt so? And others say, it is only shamming we do, as also the New Quay people. Others scoff, and make light of these spiritual things. But thanks to God, He knows our very thoughts, and that it is from our very souls we do this work. There is a great revival awakening in the near future. Satan has mustered all his regiments, for this is a sign of danger to his kingdom, and tonight we are going to hold a revival meeting at Capel Drindod. Oh! We do hope that God will pour His Spirit abundantly upon us tonight. There will be a great concourse of young people there. I wish if it were practicable to come with these meetings to Loughor. I intend to write a letter to Moriah's Young Men's Prayer Meeting, as to how to prepare and receive this great blessing. I am waiting to see what the near future will bring to me.

I have not done much work since I am here. I try to shake off these thoughts—spiritual thoughts. But it would have been as easy to turn back the flow of the sea. This week I have done a good bit, but not as I should do. If I don't awake myself before long, the 'Education Committee' will call me to the bar, and say, 'Now, young man, you must double your energy.' I have some weeks before Christmas, and I trust before then I can do a good deal of work. I am happy, and more than happy. I possess some unspeakable joy—night and day.[69]

The young ladies from New Quay when they pray are so earnest, so simple, and not in the least nervous.[70]

I am here in very good health, and these good old people act as mothers to us. They have no other people to care for. I am afraid they will spoil us, for they are so tender-hearted, and they also share with us their dainties. In fact, they are too liberal. They are so clean and jovial.[71]

Sydney is a fine fellow. He does all the shopping. I have nothing to do but live like a gentleman. I tell him I must leave him something in my will, for he is so kind, gentle and obliging.[72]

Before I came to Newcastle Emlyn, I never met young ladies who could and were willing to speak of religious things. The old fashion was to draw a long face when speaking of religious things. But it was most part of it hypocrisy, and based on the fact and thought that God is a solemn and just God, and at the same time forgetting that God is a happy God and a joyful God. Therefore, we must be happy and joyful. Now, when we speak of religion we are full of joy, and our faces are lit up with joy. Shake off this death-like solemnity, and be joyful, ever joyful. We must show the world that we are happy, because of this blessed assurance of salvation. The old story was,

'I hope I am saved,' while we can say, 'I know I am saved.' Isaiah says, 'And the Lord laid upon Him the iniquity of us all.' Now, if the Lord has laid all our sins on Jesus, there is no sin remaining to place on us. Now, then, this question, Do you believe that God placed all your sins on Christ? Well, then, there is no sin on you; you are free, and if you are free you have life. 'If the Son therefore shall make you free, ye shall be free indeed.'[73]

ASSURANCE
INSIGHT—THEOLOGY

Assurance of salvation became a main theme in the message of the 1904 Revival. Evan Roberts himself had not always possessed such a certainty of salvation, even after his conversion at 13 years of age. He remembered some years previous to the revival attending a mission meeting held by one of the Joshua brothers at nearby Gorseinon. When the meeting was tested and those who were assured of their acceptance by God were asked to stand, Roberts remained seated.[74]

The Joshua brothers regularly emphasised this aspect of faith before, during and after the revival, an emphasis that sometimes led to public controversy in meetings.

At Cardigan, just a few miles from Newcastle Emlyn, Seth Joshua had stated that 'all who loved Jesus were sure of eternal life'. He was interrupted by a minister who 'considered himself a Christian but he could not say that he was certain of eternal life and no one else could say so'.[75]

But thousands convinced by the fruit of God's love expressed in His willingness to forgive completely saw assurance as a perfectly logical step, the outcome of simple *faith* and possession of it a badge of salvation to be permanently displayed.

Included in Evan Roberts' four prerequisites for receiving the baptism of the Spirit were a knowledge of past sins forgiven and dealt with, and a public confession of one's love for Christ. There seemed to be little room for uncertainty in that equation.

Summarising Evan Robert's revival message in March 1905, one minister notes Roberts' belief in:

1. The greatness of the saving ability of the Redeemer;
2. That no one was too much of a sinner to be made into a new creature in Christ;
3. Salvation could be instantaneous;
4. New life.

Those who responded to this for the first time found it hard to understand how anyone else could lack spiritual certainty, which sometimes led many, young converts especially, to doubt other people's salvation if assurance was absent. This negative overreaction on the part of a few, though, mustn't cloud the fact that thousands of newly converted and long-standing believers expressed an assurance of faith that led to a peace, joy and zeal that transformed their spiritual experience.

TESTIMONY OF RACHEL PHILLIPS, BETHEL CHAPEL SUNDAY MORNING, 30 OCTOBER 1904 INSIGHT—WITNESS

Roberts sat Sunday morning in a pew close to me. That was a Sunday morning to be remembered. It would never go out of my mind. There was some silent influence in the service, touching the strings of the heart. I could not restrain from weeping throughout the service, and the people, especially the young, felt this influence. I could not see the face of Roberts; those who could see it told me his face was shining, his countenance was changing, and appeared as if under a wonderful influence. When going out, and before going down the steps of the gallery, he stood and looked at us saying, 'Well, what a meeting! Oh, dear! The place is full of the influence of the Holy Spirit! Oh, I felt it coming over me like a breeze!' When descending the steps, the world came in and troubled me, and I said to Roberts, 'How can I go home? My eyes are red because of weeping in the service.' His answer was, 'Never mind; do not be afraid to show that you feel. Come home.'[76]

TESTIMONY OF RACHEL PHILLIPS SUNNYSIDE, SUNDAY AFTERNOON, 30 OCTOBER 1904

After having returned from the young people's prayer meeting after school, we could do nothing but sigh. When tea was over, Roberts said, 'Let us have a prayer meeting—iron sharpeneth iron.' 'No', said I, 'we are going to sing an anthem and a chant tonight, and we must go to the singing practice.' I feared he was going too far and doing himself harm. If I knew as much as I do now, I would have left the anthem and chant go. I am sorry to this day that I gave more importance to the chant and the anthem than to Evan Roberts' prayer meeting. But God knows what burdened us was care for his mental condition.' [77]

Sunday Night 30 October 1904

As I sat in the chapel *in the 6.00pm service, the Spirit brought the case of our young people before me so powerfully that it was impossible to me to keep my mind from it. It was so for half an hour. I had to pray three times for quietness.* I could not fix my mind upon the service, for always before my eyes I saw, as in a vision, the schoolroom in my own village. And there, sitting in rows before me, I saw my old companions and all the young people, and I saw myself address them. I shook my head impatiently, and strove to drive away this vision, but it always came back. And I heard a voice in my inward ear as plain as anything saying, 'Go and speak to these people.' And for a long time I would not. But the pressure became greater and greater and I could hear nothing of the sermon. *I would lose the minister, seeing only his form.* Then at last I could resist no longer, and I said, 'Well, Lord, if it is Thy Will, I will go.' *Having returned from the meeting I told Mr Phillips that I failed to have quietness in chapel and I asked whether it was the Spirit or the devil that was working. Mr Phillips said unhesitatingly, 'Oh, the Holy Spirit was working, and it will be beneficial for you and them [the young people of Loughor] to be together for a week.'*[78]

The Spirit has given me an earnest of a blessed future amongst our young people at Moriah. And Oh! what two meetings we had yesterday—one in the vestry and the other in Mr Phillips' house. We have not had anything like them. I have been asking God whether it would be better for some to come to Loughor with me, but He did not answer in the affirmative. [Sydney] Evans stays here, being that some things are not as we should like.[79]

SYDNEY EVANS' TESTIMONY
SUNDAY EVENING, 30 OCTOBER 1904
INSIGHT—WITNESS

The both of us were without preaching engagements that Sunday. Evan Phillips was the preacher in Bethel, and the both of us sat in the gallery in the seats reserved for the students. Evan Phillips began by preaching a short English message, reading it without ceremony from his notes. He then came to the Welsh text ... a very striking text and one through which Evan [Roberts] received the call. Here is the text, 'Oh, Father, the hour has come. Glorify Your Son.' The old patriarch then paraphrased the text, 'Oh Father, let me go. Let me take the plunge.' And I believe that it was in that text and in that paraphrase of it that Evan received the call ... He forgot everything about the service. His mind was back with the young people in Moriah till the end of the sermon. Then the meeting having finished and just before we got up out of our seats, he turned to me and said, 'I am going home tomorrow. I must go and tell the young people of Moriah what I myself have experienced, what I myself have felt.'[80]

ANNE PHILLIPS, SUNNYSIDE
INSIGHT—WITNESS

Sunday evening after coming home, and Roberts with us, we found ourselves in a great prayer meeting in the house; and this was Roberts' prayer: 'Oh, Lord, I am willing to shed my blood for Thy Son.' His words burned our bosoms, and we felt that he was shedding his blood as it were for Jesus at the time. When departing for his lodgings, he told us that he was going home on the morrow, because of the vision in the service and the call of the Spirit. We were not at all willing for him to go. There was such a charm in his company, and such divine fervour characterised him, that attracted us all.[81]

Monday 31 October 1904

I am on my way home for a week to work with our young people. The reason for this is the command of the Holy Spirit. He gave the command last night at the meeting. I could not concentrate my thoughts on the work of the service. I prayed and prayed, so that I could follow the service, but of no avail. My thoughts were wandering, and my mind riveted on our young folk at Moriah. There seemed a voice, as if it said, 'You must go, you must go!' I then told Mr Phillips about it, and I asked whether it was the devil or the Spirit. Therefore, I have decided to obey, and I feel as if the Spirit testifies of the blessed future. Consequently, I am going this morning by the 10.45.[82]

Moriah Loughor

6 LOUGHOR

Monday 31 October 1904

There will be a great change at Loughor in less than a fortnight. We are going to have the greatest revival that Wales has ever seen. We must believe God at His word. His promises we have, and why do we not believe Him? There will be wonderful things here before the end of the week.[1]

My arrival up here was unexpected; but still it has been fruitful in blessings. I began a family altar here this evening. In the afternoon I went up to see Mr Francis, but he was not at home.[2]

I saw my own minister, and I told him also. And he said that I might try and see what I could do, but that the ground was stony, and the task would be hard. I asked the young people to come together, because I wanted to talk to them.[3]

The beginning of the meetings has been grand. There were 18 (including me) in Monday night's meeting.[4]

I explained to them the object of the mission. Then I told them of the work the Spirit was and is doing at New Quay and Newcastle Emlyn, and urged them to prepare for the baptism of the Holy Spirit.[5]

I stood up to talk to them, and, behold, it was even as I had seen it in the church at Newcastle Emlyn. The young people sat as I had seen them sitting, altogether in rows before me, and I was speaking to them even as it had been shown to me. At first they did not seem inclined to listen: but I went on, and at last the power of the Spirit came down.[6]

I opened the service by explaining my object, and showing how to get the Spirit. The Spirit was clearly helping me. I prayed three times during the service.[7]

Sixteen stood up to confess Christ. Praise Him! The other was a little girl, the Spirit is working with power. We came out of the meeting at 10.00pm, and no one was tired. One very young woman remarked, 'I thought it was only 9.00pm.' Very good. The testimony of others was, 'We have never had such meetings before.' [8]

The Spirit's influence is already powerful over these people.[9]

Now this is the plan I have taken under the guidance of the Holy Spirit. There are four things to be right.

1. If there is some sin or sins in the past *not* confessed, we cannot have the Spirit. Therefore, we must search, and ask the Spirit to search us.
2. If there is something doubtful in our life, it *must* be removed—that is, something of which we are unsure as to its being wrong or right. This thing *must be* removed.
3. Total surrender to the Spirit. We *must* do and *say* all He asks us.
4. Public confession of Christ.

These are the four things leading us to the grand blessing.[10]

Six came out for Jesus. But I was not satisfied. 'Oh, Lord,' I said 'give me six more—I must have six more!' And we prayed together. At last the seventh came, and then the eighth and the ninth together, and after a time the tenth, and then the eleventh and last of all came the twelfth also. But no more. And they saw that the Lord had given me the second six, and they began to believe in the power of prayer.[11]

Tuesday 1 November 1904

Satan gave me a great deal of trouble. He asked me what need was there for me to come up from Newcastle Emlyn to Loughor to hold revival meetings, while there were plenty of ministers. Why should I waste time?[12]

We had a glorious meeting in Pisgah. Six more confessed. So, 23 have confessed, and one young girl that was not a member before. The service was left in the Spirit's hand, and by taking careful note I saw that which the Spirit wished to teach, namely *obedience*. No one tired. Praise Him![13]

Number of public confessions: six.[14]

It was late when I arrived home from David Jones' house—about 12.00— they had held the service. Mary read, and Dan prayed. My sister is going to erect a family altar.[15]

Wednesday 2 November 1904

We hope to get new testimonies tonight. Mary has begun to pray. Chester Morgan was better after confessing. Alice Gray was weeping throughout the meeting. Very good. Yea, and praise God. The *power* of the blood! David Jones said he was able to live better on Tuesday after confessing. And, Tuesday morning for the first time in his lifetime, he had to fall on his knees by the chair on the hearth. His wife, too, could not keep from praying. Praise Him! Praise Him![16]

I had a letter this morning from New Quay. Nothing but good news. Another sister has broken out again, and it was glorious there.[17]

I tried to speak to some other young people in another church, and asked them to come. But the news had gone out, and the old people said, 'May we not come too?' And I could not refuse them. So they came, and they kept on coming.[18]

Francis and his wife have been twice, and both have confessed Christ. I called with him. I intended to stay only three or five minutes, but I was obliged to stay over three hours, and the Spirit gave me strength to speak almost without a break throughout this time. Francis is under deep feeling. We had a meeting there. I prayed. Francis followed in broken feelings. After this, I asked God to give strength to the sister to pray. Our prayer was answered at once. She engaged in prayer. She prayed gloriously. After this, I gave thanks to God in prayer for the meeting.[19]

Number of public confessions: four.[20]

Our family has had a grand change. We have had a family altar this week for the first time. This again is the work of the Spirit. And last Wednesday evening, before the meeting, while I was away from home, they held a prayer meeting at home; and father for the first time prayed in their hearing. Another proof of the grand work. My sister, a girl of 16, who before was a sarcastic and peevish girl, has had a grand change, and her testimony is that she is happy now, and that there is some joy in living. You can see the change in her face.[21]

Thursday 3 November 1904

In the society Mr David Davies called upon me to take charge of the meeting. Now, I was at a loss what to do. I asked the Spirit to lead us. Then I called upon someone to begin the service. John Hughes came forward. Now before Davies had called upon me, I had asked John Hughes to begin without being called by anyone; and I promised to pray for him. Talk of praying—that was praying. The Spirit was with him in power—extraordinarily so. I then stood up to catechise the children in their verses. Upon this Mr Jones (Minister) came in. He had been to the monthly meeting. After hearing their verses, I gave the children the message I received from the Spirit. This is the message. The children were to learn this prayer, 'Send the Spirit to Moriah for Jesus Christ's sake.' They soon learned it willingly. I then asked them if they would pray this prayer night and morning. Answer, 'Yes.' 'Will you teach this prayer to the children who are absent?' 'Yes.' That was a society, in which silence reigned, boy! There's attention! There's effect! And, Oh! What a large gathering, and all because the Spirit was working. These meetings are talked of in Brynteg Church. And Thomas Shepard has been convinced. I believe Tommy is to be an instrument in the Spirit's hand to set Brynteg on fire. I have spoken to him twice. The first time I spoke to him the tears came into his eyes, and he said, 'Excuse my crying.' 'Oh,' said I, 'Never mind at all. We are familiar with tears.'[22]

I had a vision. Here it is. Near me I could see a candle burning, and casting its light around. Far away in the distance, I could see a sun rising. And, Oh! What a sight it was. Not a winter nor an autumn sun, nor the sun of spring, but the sun of a summer's morn. Well, there was something divine in it. Its beams were like long arms, extending across the heavens. And the candle continued to burn. There were three or four inches of the candle unburnt. What is the meaning of this? It is quite simple. Day is at hand. This is the beginning of a revival. But, Oh! The great sun of the revival is near at hand.[23]

Now, it is only as candlelight. But, *ere long*, we shall have the powerful *light* and *heat* of the sun. It was not a dream, but a *vision*. There have been signs also in heaven. And our bedroom has been filled many times with darkness—God filling the place. Experience—sometimes cold, sometimes fervent, sometimes I can weep, sometimes laughing and crying. Last Monday I could weep at the words, 'Calvary', 'Jesus'. These words could melt me. Now, I feel rather cool. I don't feel that Jesus is very close to me. I went to think and read of His love and sacrifice, and asked the Spirit to reveal Christ.[24]

Well, after we had had ten to confess Christ, I was not satisfied with the meeting, and I asked Jesus for another ten. Now, is it strange we had ten and only ten! A direct answer to prayer. I know God answers prayer; I can *prove* God answers prayer; this moment, I believe ... The service finished about 11.00pm.[25]

Number of public confessions: 20. We are on the eve of the greatest revival the world has ever seen![26]

Friday 4 November 1904

We began at 7.00pm and finished at 10.00pm; and asked all who had confessed Christ to remain. Then the Spirit came close to us. After I had prayed, many of the people rose and went home, but about 20 remained. And we had a testimony meeting—praising the blessed Spirit for His wonderful work. This meeting finished or rather closed at 11.30pm. And we could stay there all night.[27]

Thomas Shephard was weeping and crying aloud like a child, when I related the account of the work of the Holy Spirit, and at the thought of his own pitiable condition. There were three young men from Brynteg, one from Horeb, and some from Penuel, at Moriah. I cannot and desire not to prevent them ... I said that this was to be a meeting for young people. But the old people came too. Francis and his wife have been twice, and both have confessed Christ.[28]

In the meeting—scene—two horses, one white, the other red. Both were galloping together.[29]

Number of public confessions: 19.[30]

Saturday 5 November 1904

I am from home from morn till night, and there is no thought of going to bed before one or two o'clock in the morning. It is good to have quiet to speak of these things with calmness and freedom, and not have to be like mice watching the cats. At the beginning of the week, Mary, my sister, was going to bed before I came home, but now, the bed is out of the question until I arrive, and she does not think of going to bed until I go, lest she lose these glorious things. And, oh! I am glad of the letter I had from Mr Williams, the guard. It gives me great strength to think that so many are praying on my behalf ...

I have been to Loughor after writing the above. I have been a blessing, and have been blessed since then. I got one boy to promise to pray for his father— he and his two little brothers. The blessing I had was this—a gypsy accosted me with these words, 'Good evening, sir.' The word 'Sir' went to my heart. I answered 'Good evening' only, when I ought to have said, 'Good evening, madam.' I felt a wave of love for my fellow men flowing into my soul. And now, when I meet them, I address them as 'Sir' and 'Madam'. Praise God. I passed the football field, and I said, 'Oh! That God would thunder over their heads' ...

A glorious week, the Spirit working with power. This is the plan: We begin by asking someone to read, another to give out a hymn, and another to pray. Then I say a few words. This is what is said every night:

1.   We must confess before God every sin in our past life that has not been confessed.
2.   We must remove anything that is doubtful in our lives.
3.   Total Surrender. We must say and do all that the Spirit tells us.
4.   Make a public confession of Christ.

That is the plan that the Spirit revealed to me. Sixty-five have stood up to confess Christ, and the effect in their lives is, some strange joy within them, their lives are purer, and a desire to say more of Jesus, and do more for Him. This is the song of the girls now—religion. Religion from morn till night. Many of the differences that people had between themselves have been removed. [31]

This has been a blessed week. I have been very busy. Off from morning till late at night. We never go to bed this week till about one or two in the morning. I feel it so hard to leave off the things the Lord has done here.

Young girls, who were very talkative, have been roused from their indifference, and have begun to be serious. The great feature of this work is that people are being awakened, and learning to *obey*. Those who have been with religion have had quite a new and blessed experience. They never thought what joy there was in an open confession of Christ. Young people from the Independents and Baptists come to these meetings. Of course, I cannot stop them, and I do not want to stop them. I should like very much if the Spirit was to descend on other denominations.

I intend returning to Newcastle Emlyn next Tuesday, unless I will respond to Mr Francis' desire. He wants me to stay for a week at his church. I have not had an answer from God yet. I must obey His calling. I want to learn my lessons, and prepare for college. And also I want to work for my Friend and Saviour. This fire is burning in me; and I am willing to do His command. I believe a grand revival is close at hand in the near future.

The service finished at twenty minutes past twelve. [32]

Sunday 6 November 1904

We have had the Spirit with us throughout this last week; tonight three girls and one man were baptised by the Holy Spirit. Oh! It was a meeting full of awe. Every person present was praying this prayer: 'Send the Holy Spirit now, for Jesus Christ's sake.'

This was a 'Circle Prayer'—each one had to pray. Oh! The effect was marvellous. And while the prayer was going on, one of our young men was filled with the Spirit. Praise Him! Yes! Yes! When this had gone around, we began again— this time with the addition 'more powerfully'—'Send the Spirit now more powerfully, for Jesus Christ's sake.'

All our children at Moriah are every night and morning praying this beautiful prayer given to me by the Holy Spirit: 'Send the Spirit to Moriah, for Jesus Christ's sake' ...

Oh! I am quite happy this week and throughout the last. But, nevertheless, it has been a grand fight with the tempter. But, thanks be to God, I am now a conqueror. He tried to destroy my faith ... by saying: What did I want at Loughor while there are so many ministers to be had? Why did I waste my time? And then he said that God's Spirit was not with me, and that these grand effects were only the results of my relating the signs and visions I had seen.[33]

I know not what to write. I am almost too full. My heart is full, and brimming over with joy. The Holy Spirit descended in power at Moriah tonight—or rather Monday morning—between twelve and one o'clock. I am *certain* of *four* who have been baptised, and I am not absolutely sure about *one* other person. It

is likely that she, too, has been abundantly blessed. These are the persons:-
(1) David Jones (Daniel's brother); (2) Alice Gray; (3) Catherine, my sister;
(4) Elizabeth Rees (Phrampton Road); (5) Miss Harries (William Harries' sister).
I am not quite certain about the last, but she said she felt rather full, and
that she could not contain more—but many have felt so.

It was a wonderful and awful meeting. The service was closed at ten minutes
past one. The services finish later and later as they proceed. Monday night,
Tuesday night and Wednesday night, a little past ten; Thursday night, about
eleven o'clock; Friday night, half-past eleven; Saturday night, twenty minutes
past twelve; Sunday night, ten minutes past one (or, rather, Monday morning).
And by the end of this week we shall be staying until daybreak! One thing
that gives me great joy is the fact that so many from the other denominations
come to us, and some from the Established Church. Very good. Yes, they too
need the fire.

The results of last week's work are almost incredible. Peace has been made
between many. The girls that used to talk in chapel during the service have
become serious. All day Sunday everything was as silent as the grave; 'the
children', to use Mr Hammon's phrase, 'as quiet as angels'. Many muddy pools
have been disturbed by the flow of this new water.

The effects of the confessing are marvellous. Peace has been made between
many. A large number have already confessed. And Hugh Jones has confessed.
He was backsliding. But I rejoice that he has been caught by the Spirit. 'Since
50 years ago,' said Hugh, 'I have never seen anything like it. And I hope now
that I shall have strength to hold to the end.' Some have stood up to confess
Christ for the first time, and they feel they have some joy never experienced
before. For instance, at the close of Sunday morning's service. I asked if

anyone was desirous of confessing Christ. Two of the sisters stood up, Mrs Edwards (John Edwards' widow) and Mrs Parry Davies (Mary Parry). And in the evening service, she said she felt better since the morning service. And last night, I went about asking some if they desired to confess Christ, and trying to help them a little. During this time, Mary Parry was on her feet, handkerchief in hand, leading the singing—the people, it seems, singing too slowly to please her. Before, she was quiet and retired, but she is completely changed. Praise God. I can scarcely do anything now, but praise Him.

Some lad stood up last night to confess Christ—a lad who had a marked impediment in his speech. And, Oh! What an effect he had on the congregation. He was asking, 'P-p-p-p-r-r-r-ay-ay-f-f-f-o-o-o-o-r-r-m-m-m-m-me.' There's an effect. The place streamed with tears. 'Pray for me.' And pray I did that moment that God would answer him and baptise him with the Holy Spirit. After the service had continued until it was twelve o'clock. I said I was not satisfied with it, and that we must get the blessing, even if it were necessary to stay down until daybreak. I said that we would have to 'strive with heaven'. Then the people came down from the gallery, and sat close to one another. 'Now,' said I, 'we must *believe* that the Spirit will come; not think He will come; not hope He will come; but *firmly believe* that He will come.' Then I read the promises of God, and pointed out how definite they were. (I am doing all under the guidance of the Holy Spirit, and praise be to Him.) After this, the Spirit said that *everyone* was to pray. Pray now, not confess, not sing, not give experiences, but pray and believe, and wait. And this is the prayer, 'Send the Spirit now, for Jesus Christ's sake.' The people were sitting, and only closed their eyes. The prayer began with me. Then it went from seat to seat—boys and girls—young men and maidens. Some asking in silence, some aloud, some coldly, some with warmth, some formally, some in tears, some with difficulty, some adding to it, boys and girls, strong voices, then tender voices.

Oh, wonderful! I never thought of such an effect. I felt the place beginning to be filled, and before the prayer had gone halfway through the chapel, I could hear some brother weeping, sobbing, and saying, 'O dear, dear.' 'Well, well.' 'O dear, dear.' On went the prayer, the feeling becoming more intense; the place being filled more and more. I then went to see the brother, and who should it be but David Jones! 'What is the matter?' said I, 'Oh! he answered, 'I have had something wonderful.' After this, he said that he felt his heart was too large for his bosom. I told him, 'There, you have had the Holy Spirit.' 'I hope so,' said he. The prayer had then ended its *journey*, but not its message. 'Shall we ask again for more?' 'No,' said David Jones. He had had as much as he could hold. But there were others, who had not had enough, and I said that brother Jones had had enough, but that we could go on to ask for more, and that Jones could ask God to withhold, if necessary. God can give and withhold.

Then we added to the prayer, 'Send the Spirit more powerfully, for Jesus Christ's sake.' The prayer begins its journey. And, Oh! With what effect! The Spirit was coming nearer and nearer all the while. On this journey, the Spirit descended upon two sisters. And, Oh! It descended with power! They were shouting aloud—shouting as I never heard anyone shout before. The prayer was not allowed to end its journey around. The people were in a circle around them. There was a sight! The people looked amazed and terrified, while I smiled, saying, 'Oh, there is no danger.' After a few minutes, the two sisters regained their composure, and Catherine said, 'Sing now.' And 'Praise Him' was sung, but I fear there was but little real praising, for the people were so amazed at the sight. Then some young brother began to sing 'May Thy blessing.' And the meeting came to a close. And on the way out, Elizabeth Rees broke out into weeping, being filled with the Spirit, and would have fallen had not some of the friends held her. I know not what the end of this week will be.

I intend staying here for another week. Mr Francis beseeches me not to go back upon any account, since that would only be leaving good work half done. This will be the plan this week—everyone to pray individually for the Spirit— 'Send the Spirit *now*, for Jesus Christ's sake.'

A 'Young Women's Prayer Meeting' was formed in Moriah on Sunday afternoon. I was alone with them. I would have been glad to have David Jones. But the Spirit said I had better not. Every one of them prayed—about 25 girls—asking Him to bless the meeting, or asking for the Spirit, or praising Him. There will be a glorious place here before long.[34]

MARY ROBERTS, QUALITON RECORD INSIGHT—WITNESS

We were all quite surprised when Evan arrived home on that Monday morning. It was only Saturday that I'd received a letter from him and he said nothing about coming home; just that he couldn't concentrate on his studies but hoped to do so before the end of the year. Mother thought that he had been preaching somewhere on the Sunday and that he was calling in on his way back. He went on to explain that he had come home for the whole week because he had had an incredible experience and wanted the young people who he used to meet with in Moriah at 9:30 every Sunday morning for an hour before the meeting to be led in the same experience that he had had. This was the meeting for young men who Evan sought to encourage to take part in public prayer.

Interviewer—Something quite incredible happened that morning?

When Evan came home Dan was lying on the couch and looking somewhat down and depressed. Evan couldn't understand what was wrong until Dan told him that he was losing his sight. It was pitiful to see Dan as he went to read the Bible and finding himself unable to read a word. He had been to a specialist in Llanelli and was given no hope. He had not told Evan about this until then because he hadn't wanted Evan to worry about him. But when he heard he said to Dan, 'You will have your sight. You are needed by the Lord.' Suddenly Dan received his sight, a sort of miracle had taken place. And when he revisited the specialist, he was amazed and was unable to understand what had happened. He never again had any more trouble with his eyes.

On Monday afternoon Evan went to see the minister to get the elders' permission to hold young people's meetings after the prayer meeting on a Monday night. He received permission and in that meeting he shared some of his experience and it was evident to all that he had experienced something quite incredible. Then he explained the way of blessing to us all. First one had to confess all sins. Second everything doubtful had to be forsaken (put to one side). Third one must confess Jesus. Fourth one must give instant obedience to the Holy Spirit.

Sixteen got up to confess the Lord Jesus as Saviour on Monday night. Six got up Tuesday night at Pisgah, the school room where Evan had been a superintendent over the years. Then on Wednesday night 20 got up and so on, on Thursday night, Friday night, Saturday night. Then on Sunday night a meeting was held after the usual one. That lasted until eleven o'clock. Then Evan asked all who had confessed Jesus during the week to stay behind. The doors were shut and Evan proceeded to give us prayer. 'Oh. send the Holy Spirit now, for the sake of Jesus Christ!'

But before half the congregation had prayed the prayer the place was ablaze— that's the most incredible meeting I've ever been to. People sighing under the weight of the burden of their sins, some confessing while others were praying, 'Stay your hand, oh great Jesus, I can take no more.'

Monday 7 November 1904

... went to bed today at 3.15. It is improving.[35] The Spirit descended on a few Sunday night, then on more Monday night.[36] This is bending ... wonderful ... not just bending in the Judgement but now—bend us Lord![37]

Tuesday 8 November 1904

Oh there's a hard time—praying fervently until four o'clock in the morning with no visible result.[38]

Some of us were in agonies for nine hours and yet the Spirit didn't descend; the people were disobedient ... He will not come to stubborn people.[39]

Wednesday 9 November 1904

Brynteg was full to overflowing, the chapel could not contain all the people. There's a happy meeting! The Spirit was there in power. Daniel Davies, grocer, was filled. And, Oh! There's a sight! He came down to the big pew to me, and said, 'Something strange has come over me.' I told him that he had received the Spirit. And, Oh! There was a sight after this! He laid hold of me as though he were beside himself, and kissed me. And then he laid hold of me and his wife. The majority of the people were on their feet, singing with spirit 'Praise Him'. Davies wanting them to be silent that he might say a word, but it was impossible. Then they ceased. And he said, 'Oh, here's a new man.' Mrs Ann Saunders received the baptism the same time. And in truth I know not how many have had it this week. Miss Clarke has been bent, and Miss Watkins (Mrs Francis' sister). Francis is about to receive it. Pray for him. [Mr] Lewis, of Libanus Chapel, Pontardulais, desires me to come there for a night. But I cannot go there this week. I may be able next week, if the Spirit leads me. A request has come from Ammanford, too, for me to go there for a night.

I do not intend coming to school this term. I have not time to do any schoolwork at home. We may possibly have to go through Wales. If we shall, heaven be praised. This is a jolly time. I am quite contented, perfectly happy; plenty of work from morn till night. I am working nights now:

Sunday, from 9.00am to 1.10am—16 hours
Monday night, from 7.00pm to 3.00am—8 hours
Tuesday night, from 7.00pm to 4.00am—9 hours
Wednesday night, from 7.00pm to 3.00am—8 hours[40]

This has been the order of our meetings:

Sunday night, from 6.00pm to 1.00am—7 hours
Monday night, from 7.00pm to 3.00am—8 hours
Tuesday night, from 7.00pm to 4.00am—9 hours
Wednesday night, from 7.00pm to 3am—8 hours ...[41]

One of our deacons [at Moriah Chapel] was filled, he came on to me and embraced me, *and kissed me*, while many of the congregation stood on their feet and on the benches, and Oh! What joy! He was clapping his hands, and saying, '*Diolch iddo*' ('Thanks be to Him'), and laughing. You could think that he was mad—for he was mad with joy. From ten to 20 were filled last night. And Sydney is coming home next week.[42]

On Tuesday night He did not seem to have descended upon anyone, but oh, wonderful! He descended very powerfully on Wednesday night.[43]

Thursday 10 November 1904

The place of worship is crammed to door and lobby. Now, the Spirit told me to say that *three* things show that God is with us:

1.   Enormous congregations;
2.   The union of the different denominations;
3.   The baptism of the Holy Spirit.

People come to see and hear *'The insane fellow'*. Thanks be to God that the *'insane fellow'*, in the hands of the Spirit, has been the means to throw down many castles of sin. Glory to God! No! I am not insane—but filled with the Spirit.

Now, we must pray for the spread of this grand revival.

I have been asked to come to Pontardulais, a place four miles away. And also to a place ten miles away, called Ammanford. It was through Mr Jenkins, New Quay, that the fire was kindled at this place [Ammanford].
Everyone in the meeting *must* pray.

1. Send the Spirit now for Jesus Christ's sake.
2. Send the Spirit now powerfully for Jesus Christ's sake.
3. Send the Spirit more powerfully for Jesus Christ's sake.
4. Send the Spirit still more powerfully for Jesus Christ's sake.

I was speaking last night to a young man, and he told me his very besetting sin. He could not and would not tell it to any other person. Now, I can pray God to remove that very sin. And I am sure God will do so.[44]

What a service! The girls and the women shouting aloud, having forgotten themselves. Over 30 were baptised by the Holy Spirit. There's a band of workers! The meetings go on far into the night—or rather into the day. We came home this morning at 4.15. Very good. Yes! Yes! Oh! Yes! The people say that the boy is foolish—that he is insane!!! Nay! Nay! Heaven be praised. The people come to us from a long distance. I am thankful that Christ through the Holy Spirit draws people to Him. Little girls of 12 and 13 are receiving the Spirit ...

I saw Rachel Phillips on Thursday, and I went with her to Landore. The young women praying in Brynteg last night—Mag is good—very good. They were heart rending, and heaven be praised for them.[45]

WESTERN MAIL REPORT OF MEETING HELD ON THURSDAY 10 NOVEMBER 1904 INSIGHT—WITNESS

The meeting at Brynteg Congregational Chapel on Thursday night was attended by those remarkable scenes which have made previous meetings memorable in the life history of so many of the inhabitants of the district. The proceedings commenced at seven o'clock and they lasted without a break until 4:30 o'clock this (Friday) morning. During the whole time the congregation were under the influence of deep religious fervour and exaltation. There were about 400 people present when I took my seat in the chapel, about 9 o'clock. The majority of the congregation were females ranging from young misses of 12 to matrons with babies in their arms.

Mr Roberts is a young man of rather striking appearance. He is tall and distinguished-looking and with an intellectual air about his clean-shaven face. His eyes are piercing and their brightness and the pallor of his countenance seemed to suggest that these nightly vigils are telling upon him. There was however no suggestion of fatigue in his conduct of the meeting. There is nothing theatrical about his preaching. He does not seek to terrify his hearer, and the eternal torment finds no place in his theology. Rather does he reason with the people and show them by persuasion a more excellent way. I had not been many minutes in the building before I felt that this was no ordinary gathering. Instead of the set order of proceedings to which we are accustomed at the orthodox religious service, everything here was left to the spontaneous impulse of the moment. The preacher too, did not remain in his usual seat. For the most part he walked up and down the aisles, open Bible in one hand, exhorting one, encouraging another, and kneeling with a third to implore a blessing from the throne of grace.

A young woman rose to give out a hymn, which was sung in deep earnestness. While it was being sung several people dropped down in their seats as if they had been struck, and commenced crying for pardon. Then from another part of the chapel could be heard a resonant voice of a young man reading a portion of Scripture. While this was in progress from the gallery came an impassioned prayer from a woman crying aloud that she had repented her ways, and was determined to live a better life henceforward. All this time Mr Roberts went in and out among the congregation, offering kindly words of advice to kneeling penitents. He would ask them if they believed. The reply in one instance being, 'No, I would like to believe but I can't. Pray for me.' Then the preacher would ask the audience to join him in the following prayer. *'Anfon yr Ysbryd yn awr, er mwyn Iesu Grist*, Amen' (Send the Holy Spirit for Jesus Christ's sake, Amen).

This prayer would be repeated about a dozen times by all present. Then the would-be convert would suddenly rise in triumph, 'Thank God, I have now received salvation. Never again will I walk in the way of sinners.' This declaration would create a new excitement, and the congregation would joyously sing:

Diolch iddo, Diolch iddo
Byth am gofio llwch y llawr.
Thanks be to Him, Thanks be to Him
For ever remembering the *dust* of the earth.

I suppose this occurred scores of times during the nine hours over which the meeting was protracted. A very moving feature of the proceedings was the anxiety of many present for the spiritual welfare of members of their families. One woman was heart-broken for her husband who was given to drink. She implored the prayers of the congregation on his behalf. The story told by another young woman drew tears to all eyes. She said that her mother was dead and that her father had given way to sin, so that she was indeed orphaned in the world. She had attended the meetings without feeling her position, but on the previous day, while following her domestic duties, the Spirit had come upon her, bidding her to speak. And she did speak! Her address being remarkable for one who had never spoken before in public. Yet another woman made a public confession that she had come to the meeting in a spirit of idle curiosity but that the influence of the Holy Ghost worked within her, causing her to go down on her knees in penitence. It was now long past midnight, but still there was no abatement in the fervour of the gathering. Fresh fuel was added to the religious fire by Mr Roberts, who described what had appeared to him as a vision. He said that when he was before the throne of grace he saw appearing before him a key. He did not understand the meaning of this sign. Just then, however three members of the congregation rose to their feet and said that they had been converted. 'My vision is explained,' said Mr Roberts. 'It was the key by which God opened your hearts.'

At 2.30 I took a rough note of what was then proceeding. In the gallery a woman was praying, and she fainted. Water was offered her, but she refused this, saying that the only thing that she wanted was God's forgiveness. A well-known resident then rose and said that salvation had come to him. Immediately following a thanksgiving hymn was sung, while an English prayer from a new convert broke in upon the singing. The whole congregation then fell upon their knees, prayers ascending from every part of the edifice, while Mr Roberts gave way to tears at the sight. This state of fervency lasted for about ten minutes. It was followed by an even more impressive five minutes of silence, broken only by the sobs of strong men. A hymn was then started by a woman with a beautiful soprano voice. Finally Mr Roberts announced the holding of future meetings, and at 4:25 o'clock the gathering dispersed. But even at this hour the people did not make their way back home. When I left to walk back to Llanelli, I left dozens of them on the road still discussing what is now the chief subject in their lives. They had come prepared with lamps and lanterns, the lights of which in the early hours of darkness were weird and picturesque.[46]

INSIGHT—INTERVIEW

Remarkable scenes near Llanelli
Collier's wonderful preaching
All night meeting

The whole of South Wales has been thrilled by the remarkable scenes ... Nothing like it has been witnessed within the last 20 years and for a parallel we must go back to the historic events of 1859 ....

The modern Howell Harris is about 28 [*sic*] years of age and of commanding figure. He has the eyes of an enthusiast and the tenacity of purpose and strength of will of which martyrs are made. He also believes thoroughly in himself not as a preacher or an orator, but as a humble instrument, guided and led by a higher power. This it is which explains the marvellous hold which he exercises over his hearers. He is not a great orator in the ordinary sense of the term. What cannot strike the listener, however is the tremendous fault that is in the man. Disdaining the tricks of the pulpit beater, he speaks straight out to the heart in simple language. He tells the 'old, old story' as he would to a child and instead of striking terror into the hearts of his audience he wins them over by appealing to the conscience and all that is best in man. At later stages of his meetings however when the air is charged with electricity, Mr Roberts himself becomes powerfully moved and walks up and down the aisles of the chapel in a state of ecstatic fervour.

Interview with Mr Roberts
Remarkable utterances

The editor of *Llanelli Mercury* was privileged to have a special interview with Mr Evan Roberts at his parents' home, near Broad Oak Colliery on Friday afternoon (11 November). The young missioner was full of enthusiasm for his work, but there were traces in his deathly white face of severe mental strain. The long vigils of the week had evidently told on him and the more so as he had been able to sleep but little. However there were no signs of fatigue in his conversation. He walked up and down the little room with a restlessness that told of a brain ever at work. At times he would break out into singing snatches of hymns and would suddenly stop in order to answer a question put by his interviewer.

'I saw a *Mercury* reporter at the meeting last night, I hope he enjoyed it.'

'Yes, he has brought back a glowing account of it.'

'It was magnificent, magnificent. The Spirit is working among the people and it will change their lives.'

'You are doing very good work.'

'Don't say that. I am nothing. It is not my work. It is the work of God, and I am glad to be a humble instrument in his hands.'

'Do you think the movement will spread?'

'I feel we are on the eve of the greatest revival the country has ever seen. Great things have already been done in Cardiganshire and the same holy influence is now at work here.'

'How did you come to start your work at Loughor?'

'I am here in obedience to the command of God, who had sent me here. God is working in this, and the prophecy of Joel is about to be fulfilled.'

'Is it your intention to continue in mission work?'

'I cannot tell you. I am in the hands of God, and he will direct me what to do and where to go.'

'I am afraid you are over-taxing your strength.'

'No, no, I am not. The Holy Spirit will sustain me. I was converted 13 years ago and I have been praying for the Holy Ghost ever since, and now it has come. Oh! It is glorious. What I want for the people is to know the joy of religion. Religion was never intended to make a man gloomy. It should be the happiest thing in life. Our fathers –thank God for them—were saintly men, but were gloomy and melancholy, as though their religion was a sore trial to the flesh. What they missed was the joy of our Lord. They got into a groove, and we must now get out of it. The world is vainly trying to find joy in pleasure. It will find that the only real pleasure in life is in the following our Lord and Master.'[47]

Friday 11 November 1904

I do not know how to begin writing in the midst of this divine fire. The whole place has been moved, and my heart burns within me with the Holy Spirit.

They want us to come to Ammanford and to Libanus, Pontardulais. I believe the path is open for me to work for my Saviour. The fire is spreading rapidly, and effectually.

People hold prayer meetings in the houses, the family altar is erected, and testimony meetings are held in the steel works. And that was a society meeting in Moriah Chapel (Loughor)! We had to stop the people from speaking. Praise God! What prejudice there is against the movement! Well, I have to say strange things; I have to open my mouth and speak out. And, thank heaven, those things are very effectual. The Spirit convicts powerfully. I am bound to speak the truth, be the cost what it may. It is pointed truth, nevertheless it must be said.

I have scarcely any time to correspond. There is so much work ... I am in excellent health.[48]

SOUTH WALES
Daily Post

WEDNESDAY 16 NOVEMBER 1904
INSIGHT—INTERVIEW

'The Spirit baptised me ... Afterwards it sent me a message. 'Go home for a week', it commanded. So I obeyed. I went home to Loughor. Then another message came. It told me to go forth with three women. Their names were even mentioned. I communicated the message to them. They obeyed. Two others followed.'

'But this message,' the pressman protested, 'How was it manifested?'
'God seized hold of me. He pressed me down to the earth. I felt the weight of his hand upon me, for my face was purple. My mother had the same experience when she was converted. She fell to the ground so that people thought she was ill.'

'And what are you going to do?'

'Do? How do I know? I shall go where the Spirit calls me. I have left everything. I have given up everything except £200. And I would surrender even that with pleasure. Even now I am waiting the Master's bidding. Ah! It is a grand life. I am happy, as happy that I could walk on the air. Tired? Never. God has made me strong; he has given me courage. I could face millions.'

'No wonder the ministry is attended here,' they say. 'Is a young man, a boy, preaching what?'

Mirth! Actually mirth and laughter. He smiles when he prays. He laughs when he exhorts. So Welsh ministers shake their heads. They do not understand.

Journeys of Evan Roberts

The outline of these journeys is taken from the book by R. Tudur Jones.[49]

Evan Roberts Leaves Loughor

First Journey, 13 November–24 December 1904, South Wales Valleys

Loughor, 31 October–12 November

Trecynon, 13–15 November

Pontycymmer, 16–18 November

Bridgend, 19 November

Pyle, 19 November

Abergwynfi, 19 November

Abercynon, 20 November

Mountain Ash, 21–22 November

Ynysybwl, 23–24 November

Cilfynydd, 25–26 November

Porth, 27–28 November

Treorchy, 29 November–1 December

Pentre, 2–4 December

Caerphilly, 5–6 December

Senghennydd, 7 December

Ferndale, 8–9 December

Ynyshir, 9 December

Ferndale, 10 December

Mardy, 11 December

Tylorstown, 12–13 December

Merthyr Vale, 14–15 December

Hafod, 16–17 December

Pontypridd, 18 December

Clydach Vale, 19–20 December

Tonypandy, 21 December

Penygraig and Williamston, 22 December

Treherbert, 23 December

Rest 24–28 December

Second Journey, 28 December 1904–2 February 1905, Swansea and Districts

Clydach, 28 December

Morriston, 29–30 December

Swansea, 1–4 January

Llansamlet, 5–8 January

Birchgrove, 9 January

Skewen, 10–11 January

Tonna, 12 January

Aberdulais, 13 January

Neath, 15–16 January

Resolven, 17 January

Hirwain, 18–19 January

Bedling, 20 January

Dowlais, 22–24 January

Penydarren, 25 January

Heolgerrig, 26 January

Cefn (Merthyr), 27–29 January

Merthyr, 30 January

Twynyrodyn, 31 January

Troedyrhiw, 1 February

Rest 3–7 February

Third Journey, 8–21 February 1905, Valleys

Nantymoel, 8–9 February

Ogmore Vale, 10 February

Maesteg, 12–14 February

Nantyffyllon (Maesteg), 15 February

Caera (Maesteg), 16 February

Cymmer, 17 February

Pontrhydyfen, 19 February

Cwmavon, 20–21 February

Week of silence, 23 February–1 March

Home, 4–10 March

Newcastle Emlyn, 10–13 March

Blaenannerch, 14–15 March
New Quay, 16 March
Henllan, 17 March
Newcastle Emlyn, 18–23 March
Loughor 23–25 March

Fourth Journey, 28 March–17 April 1905, Liverpool

Rest 18 April–6 June
Capel Curig, North Wales, 18 April–16 May
Gwylfa Cemais, 16 May–6 June

Fifth Journey 6 June–6 July 1905

Anglesey, 6 June–3 July
Caernarfon and Bala, 4–6 July

Sixth Journey, 15 November–2 December 1905, Valleys Revisited

Pontycymmer
Hermon
Bridgend
Pencoed
Cenfig Hill
Tylorstown
Trecynnon
Bristol

Seventh Journey, 5 December 1905–4 January 1906, Caernarfonshire

THE ENIGMA OF EVAN ROBERTS

Evan Roberts' launch from Loughor, in mid-November 1904, led to weeks of intensive evangelistic activity in the mining valleys of South Wales. Without a planned itinerary, he sought to be open to the Spirit's guidance, and visited scores of valley churches with his message of the transforming power of the cross of Christ and the joy of the Holy Spirit.

Being an instant media celebrity he was regularly mobbed by crowds of the interested and curious, all seeking to see and hear the young revivalist at first hand. Even a rumour of his arrival would cause a stir.

Loughor Station

A rumour was spread about Llanelli on Sunday that Mr Evan Roberts was at Loughor and as a result hundreds of people walked from the town and district while a large number went up by train. On their arrival they were informed that Evan Roberts was not there. Therefore they immediately started for home. Midway between Llanelli and Loughor a prayer meeting was held, one man was heard making a remark that if he had not seen Evan Roberts he gave thanks that he had seen Evan Robert's master, which was as much as he required.[1]

And there were even hoaxes.

A HOAX AT FERRYSIDE

News was circulated that Evan Roberts was coming to Ferryside on a certain Tuesday to conduct revival meetings and had written to inform the local minister, the Revd D.J. Lewis of his coming. Excitement grew at the news. In fact a good many colliers and others did not go to work as usual on Tuesday and several went down very early in the morning to Ferryside. In all some 60 persons went from Kidwelly alone (four miles away). There was very great disappointment when at noon the news was received that Evan Roberts was not coming and it subsequently transpired that the letter, which was couched in most pious terms and concluded as follows: 'Yours in Christ, Evan Roberts', was a forgery.[2]

> **HUNDREDS OF LETTERS WERE WRITTEN, INVITING THE YOUNG ELISHA TO BRING THE FIRE OF REVIVAL TO LOCALITIES ALL OVER WALES.**

Hundreds of letters were written, inviting the young Elisha to bring the fire of revival to localities all over Wales. Chapels were crowded, often within five to ten minutes of their doors opening, police being brought in to control the masses seeking to obtain entry. To stop overcrowding a number of chapels in an area were opened and quickly filled, each congregation hoping the revivalist would show his face.

Evan Roberts wasn't the only revivalist of the awakening. Joseph Jenkins and his team of young people had been active in revival mission months before in the Spring of 1904. Other nonconformist ministers, including R.B. Jones, W.W. Lewis, W.S.

Jones and Keri Evans conducted missions and conventions for the awakening and strengthening of the spiritual life of thousands. Sydney Evans and Dan Roberts, Evan's brother, also conducted missions and saw thousands come to faith. Besides these, there were countless, less well-known church leaders and young people now forgotten who spread the revival spirit by their enthusiastic sharing of its message. It was only a comparatively small percentage of converts that came to faith in and through a meeting where Evan Roberts was present.

∨ Joseph Jenkins

∧ Dan
Roberts

Yet, the personality who more than any other remains linked in the public and historic consciousness with the Welsh Revival of 1904 is that of Evan Roberts. He captured the imagination and attention of the public then, and still 100 years later continues to do so. Newspapers, periodicals, postcards, mugs and even cotton handkerchiefs carried his image during the revival months. A now extremely rare, Staffordshire figurine was produced of him, similar to the busts and figurines of other past spiritual heroes. Ever since, historians and church leaders have debated and disagreed as to the level and usefulness of his contribution to the revival. In the ongoing debate it is often pointed out that much of the publicity and hype highlighting Evan Roberts himself arose from the fact that the *Western Mail*, and other papers, concentrated their main reporting on the young revivalist and his progress, giving less attention to the other leaders. This then, it is argued, is the obvious key to his popularity. Yet this still doesn't explain why the media decided to focus their attention on Evan and not some other revivalist in the first place. What was it that drew them to him? What was the secret of this man's popularity? Why were people so interested? What was behind Evan Roberts' spiritual magnetism? Why was it that so many saw him as the personality under God that helped change a nation?

One factor that highlighted the contribution of Evan Roberts to the revival was the contrast that he presented to the contemporary religious scene. Preaching had often become formal, decorated and delivered in the best Welsh, alliteration and bardic news hiding rather than explaining Christian truth; this young man's plain, everyday vernacular messages, unadorned by learned rhetoric, were more than a welcome relief from the normal Sunday affair. The pulpit had been manned by the professional, and the prophetic was often lost in the performance, a performance rather to be enjoyed than to present a challenge.

THERE IS NO DOUBTING HIS ABSOLUTE SINCERITY AND CONVICTION.

In Evan Roberts we see the return of that prophetic element. He said what he thought, when he thought it, and how he thought it. His messages sprung from his heart—the media noted the contrast.

> He spoke for an hour and a quarter under evident restraint and in a quiet confident style. He made no attempt at rhetoric and was never at a loss for a phrase or a word ... There is no doubting his absolute sincerity and conviction.[3]

He neither preaches nor harangues; he simply talks, pleads, exalts, explains; tells his own story simply and willingly and smilingly invites ... He is evidently sincere and he prays with the fervour of a man whose heart is deeply moved.[4]

Evan rarely preached a traditional sermon, but spoke as he felt moved at different times during the meeting. Sometimes he would comment on the message of a hymn that was being sung— taking a line and applying it to the congregation. At other times he would speak on a text that may have been quoted in prayer.

> **TRUTH LEARNED AND MEMORISED WAS NOW TRUTH UNLEASHED IN THE POWER OF THE SPIRIT.**

Many were amazed at his biblical knowledge as he sought to press home his messages. The years of regular Bible studies in the mine and forge were now being utilised by the anointing of the Holy Spirit. Truth learned and memorised was now truth unleashed in the power of the Spirit.

These messages were filled with personal anecdotes illustrating how the truth had already affected him. At Birchgrove he sought to encourage those who felt that God was distant and wasn't responding to their prayer. Using the text, 'My God, my God, why hast Thou forsaken me?', he went on to share his experience.

I was going to bed one night and before going I prayed but there didn't seem to be any God answering. I prayed in the bed yet there was no answer. He had hidden His face. I got up in the morning—breakfast was on the table but I couldn't even look at it. I went out to look at nature but it had nothing to say to me. The birds were singing but I wished they would be silent. I began to wonder if I had committed a sin? No—not one! Not one! Had I left some duty or responsibility undone? No—not one! Why was God hiding His face then? Oh, only that I might appreciate the worth of that communion in His absence.[5]

His personal touch communicated to the working class as well as to others. In Evan Roberts we have someone who bypasses the orthodox and accepted religious channelling of truth. The set sermon is replaced by an informal yet passionate exposition of Christian teaching. Evan didn't preach sermons— rather he proclaimed a message, in his own words that all could understand.

There is some truth in the statement that Evan Roberts's neglect of set teaching through the usual preached word during this time weakened the overall effect of the revival. Yet there were many who felt that Evan Roberts's style of message and its apparent success was God's judgment on the preaching methods of the time. Evan might have seemed a very young apprentice when

Evan Roberts in the open air

compared to the regal preachers of his day. Yet it was this young David who got on with the giant-killing, without the traditional and often burdensome armour.

His method of conducting revival services also added to this contrast and awoke the interest of a church that was in danger of slumbering spiritually in the well-tried, unchanging and predictable methods of nineteenth-century Victorian nonconformity.

The well-educated, respectable minister, preaching in the 'splendid isolation' of his fortified pulpit was replaced by the 'not yet ordained' and unpredictable youngster who saw the whole building as his parish! He would often walk up and down the aisles, Bible in hand, encouraging converts and praying with those under conviction. Then he might lead the singing or simply stay silent while waiting for inspiration. The congregation didn't know what was going to happen next. The danger of some quiet 'shut-eye' in services received a death blow, even though the revival meetings often lasted into the early hours of the morning.

Being at a revival meeting meant that each person attending could take part in the service as well. Evan Roberts taught that the meetings were to be lead by the Spirit. They were to be undirected by people. One of his four points concerning immediate obedience to the Spirit underlines this thinking. Evan's early leading of the meetings mainly consisted of encouraging the

Congregational prayer

congregation to be led and to respond to the promptings of the Spirit. This idea so captivated him that he would often rebuke those who sought to take the reins of the meeting into their own hands. There is no doubting his early sincerity in this practice, as he himself would often stop speaking when either a soloist or member of the congregation would be led to pray. Although Evan recognised that as the revival progressed this sort of openness was liable to be misused—he began to direct and lead to a greater measure as a result— here we see a practical outworking of the doctrine of the priesthood of all believers. It wasn't the minister alone who audibly took part. Worship was a congregational activity and all could be involved in prayer, praise and encouragement. The laity were given a voice in the meeting; a principle many of them were to hold on to for the rest of their lives.

This newly enfranchised laity also included women, some of whom became a part of his mission team as he travelled around the country. During his stay at Newcastle Emlyn he had come into contact with the 'spiritually fired up' girls from New Quay and he was, to say the least, impressed. Here were girls who he saw as different, the difference being in their devotion to their Saviour. They included Florrie Evans, a young girl from Tabernacle, New Quay. Through her testimony, revival fire had been sparked in the early part of 1904.

Evan Roberts had seen these girls at revival meetings in the Newcastle Emlyn area, at Twrgwyn and Capel Drindod, during his stay at the grammar school. They were also present at the Blaenannerch meetings. Immediately following his experience at Blaenannerch he planned to go through Wales with a team of young people sharing the good news. Of the ten names that he considered to go, seven were those of women.[6] Six weeks later, when he left Loughor for his first mission, he took a team of five women with him ... Miss Priscilla Watkins (23 years old, a teacher), Miss Mary Davies (23 years old, a Sunday school teacher and popular reciter), Miss Lavinia Hooker (21 years old, a

Sydney Evans

dressmaker and soloist), Miss Mary Davies (24 years old plus, an ex-teacher) and Miss Annie May-Rees (15 years old, a Sunday school teacher, singer and musician).[7]

The team was to change in its make-up as the revival progressed, but yet its contribution to the revival meetings added a new flavour to the spirituality of the time. Generally speaking, public worship was male-dominated; few women were seen in the pulpit, or 'big seat' as the deacons' pew was called.

Evan Roberts's revival services changed this—as did those of Sydney Evans and Dan Roberts—at least during the revival itself, by incorporating these women's contributions in the services.

Beginning by singing and passing on words of personal testimony, many of  the women couldn't help passing on messages that they felt laid on their hearts. Some of the team became evangelists in their own right during the revival, conducting their own meetings and preaching their own sermons.

Annie Davies

These spiritual 'Deborahs' soon became household names, and appeared with or without Evan Roberts on the postcards of the day. The most well-known is probably Annie Davies who joined Evan's team in November 1904. Only 18 years old, with a wonderful voice and a growing confidence in her own ability as the revival progressed, she remained as Evan Roberts' main soloist throughout most of the principal revival missions. She's most well-known for her rendition of 'Here is love, vast as the ocean', which would often melt congregations, the song becoming quickly known as the love song of the revival. When asked about his team of singing soloists, Evan Roberts noted, 'They go with me wherever I go. I never part from them without feeling that something is absent if they are not there. The singing is very important, but not everything'.[8]

Four young ladies who had come under the spell of the 'Welsh Wesley', and who were not religiously disposed prior to this week, are now full of zeal and enthusiasm. One of them is a beautiful singer, and she and three others banded themselves together and made a round of the public houses and the clubs where they sang hymns and induced men who were drinking there to come to the meeting ... 'I used to go to the dance,' said one of them, 'and I thought I couldn't ever give it up, but I shall never go to a dance again!' She spoke these words at the close of the afternoon prayer meeting. Evan Roberts was there, and he was observed to be weeping like a child.[9]

While a number of people discussed the issue of women taking part publicly in the revival meetings, most welcomed the difference and appreciated the exuberance, enthusiasm and singing of these girls. As most were young, rumours abounded about Evan Roberts' relationship with them, yet they remained rumours. There is still no evidence of scandal, and a look at the itinerary of the evangelist who was daily in the public eye gave little opportunity either. The girls would always stay in separate lodgings when on

Evan and the revivalists from Loughor

mission. Yet rumours of his engagement to Annie Davies still sold papers and made interesting reading.

Evan Roberts' ground-breaking style and method made him a model for other leaders in the years following the revival. He created a mould that wouldn't be discarded rapidly, but imitated and used by fledgling Pentecostal leaders in the coming years. Evan wasn't the last breath of the nineteenth century; he was in many ways the first breath of the twentieth century. The path he cleared through years of traditional religious undergrowth soon became a well-beaten track in the history of the new Pentecostal movement's style and teaching. Evan himself became an ideal example for many of the leaders seeking to be open to the Spirit. He was seen by them as a pioneer in understanding the immanence and direct revelation of the Holy Spirit and, in the spiritual consciousness of thousands, as an icon to be imitated.

During and after the revival, newspaper stories about Evan Roberts and his methods, which had been reported in detail, became documented cameos and blueprints for thousands of other meetings throughout the principality of Wales, and wider afield. Even though these services were never visited by the revivalist himself, his methodology was copied nationally. Physically absent, yet spiritually and emotionally present through the press coverage, Evan's message and personality stamped itself on a nation within a few months.

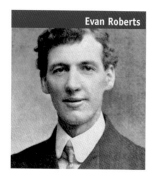

Evan Roberts

His methodology wasn't just a pleasant contrast to what preceded it; it was painfully controversial, especially his claims regarding the guidance of the Spirit. This guidance was something he relied on, not just for worship services, but for direction as to where to visit next on mission or even whether to see someone who had come to speak to him. Professor John Young Evans, who met him at his home on Monday 27 March 1905, noted his preoccupation with this.

> More than once in the course of the afternoon when he was being consulted on matters of apparently little moment, he hesitated before replying, while his lips were slightly but perceptibly convulsed. The Spirit's guidance had now become a matter from day to day and so far as his mission movements were concerned, he would henceforth require the first suggestion from the Spirit ... The increase of emphasis he now lays on the Spirit's guidance even in temporal affairs easily lent itself to satire and caricature.[10]

One writer commenting on this aspect of his personality notes: 'Everything that comes from his subconscious is regarded by Roberts as the guidance of the Spirit while everything that comes from reason or from the good advice of his friends is human counsel'.[11]

This may be an overstatement, yet it does contain some truth. As the revival progressed, Evan realised that subjective feeling by itself didn't always indicate the Spirit's guidance. In the meantime it did cause some controversy, as with the residents of Cardiff when Evan Roberts said that the Holy Spirit was saying 'No' to a visit there. The controversy filled the newspapers.[12]

> **AS THE REVIVAL PROGRESSED, EVAN REALISED THAT SUBJECTIVE FEELING BY ITSELF DIDN'T ALWAYS INDICATE THE SPIRIT'S GUIDANCE.**

Even more controversial and strange to the Church of the time were Roberts' claims to supernaturally given knowledge about people and events in the meetings that he led. An account of his revisit to Blaenannerch in March 1905 provides an interesting example. He enters a packed congregation and declares that:

there was someone at that moment denying the divine inspiration of the Bible. God wanted that person to confess. Prayers were offered by the sisters, then the evangelist again asked the man to confess. The missioner was evidently in overpowering agony, but no one spoke, the silence in the chapel being unbroken except for Mr Roberts' groans. 'God's order is that that man must honestly say he doesn't believe', was his cry. After a minute's pause, he said God had revealed that the man was standing. Dozens were standing, but nobody confessed. The scene was most pathetic [that is full of pathos], many in the front of the chapel sobbing bitterly during their prayers. 'God give me the name of the man', prayed the missioner and shortly afterwards he said, 'I know his name and age, won't he confess?' After a struggle with anxiety Mr Roberts said, 'The man's name is _____ , 23 years of age—Oh, Lord, Oh!' After '*Diolch iddo*' had been sung he said that the man need not confess now because he had changed his views'.[13]

Later on, he went on to warn those who were sceptical that God might divulge their names also and finished by saying there was somebody present who needed to make restitution to the church threefold because he had committed sacrilege.

There had been a number of other incidents similar to this previously; for instance, at Cwmafon in February 1905, where he said that there was a lost soul in the congregation and that God had prohibited him from praying for that soul. It was 'too late, too late'.[14] Similar incidents were to follow in the Liverpool mission. As previously noted, again as the revival progressed, Evan Roberts began to realise that subjective feeling in and of itself doesn't always guarantee that the Spirit is involved, and even warned people about over-reliance on feeling alone.

> **FEELING IS NOT THE FOUNDATION OF RELIGION, FAITH IS ... IT IS FAITH IN GOD THAT IS REALLY IMPORTANT ...**

Feeling is not the foundation of religion, faith is. And when feeling disappears do not think that God has gone with it ... We lose so many battles by resting on the heights and depths of feeling. It is faith in God that is really important ... The Holy Spirit doesn't tell us what to wear. etc. If He did that He would make you into less than man ... Do not put your reason to one side. Then you will not be out of control.[15]

Yet incidents such as these, as well as securing continued press coverage, also brought opposition to the revivalist from people who felt that this type of ministry had gone a step too far, being more fleshy than spiritual. A major attack had been made along these lines earlier in the year, in the 31 January edition of the *Western Mail*. This was by the Revd Peter Price, a Congregational minister at Dowlais, where Evan Roberts was accused of leading a sham revival.

Although Evan Roberts himself didn't respond to the criticism, the papers were filled with letters both accusing and defending the young revivalist. Support and sympathy for Evan remained widespread, yet not without reservation; and many Welsh denominational writers sought to suggest that Evan Roberts needed rest in order to regain his spiritual equilibrium. In Spring 1905, one writer notes:

Press coverage

Evan Roberts is now at Newcastle Emlyn where he is resting. Yet he has held some services in the locality ... These were very strange to say the least. We are certain then Mr Roberts needs to continue to take rest. The blessing we have received as a nation through him is too precious to be deprived of.[16]

Some writers have noted that such attacks affected him deeply and, as a result, 'Roberts seemed to depend more and more on direct, Spirit-inspired perception both as to the conduct of the meetings and the content of his messages'.[17]

Yet despite criticisms, most people regarded Evan Roberts as absolutely genuine. Even when they were unsure as to some of his methods, they were often deeply impressed by his manner and personality. In a fascinating article written at the time, Professor John Young Evans, a lecturer at the theological college at Trefecca, noted:

It is inconceivable ... that those who have most severely criticised the man would have done so had they enjoyed even a few minutes of his society ... He grows upon you ... He has a boyish exuberance, and yet a maturity of judgment, in naïve frankness and yet a depth of reserve. Not without some misgivings did his Dowlais hostess receive to her house one so closely connected by the public with the religious awakening lest in aught he should disillusion those who saw him day by day. No guest stood the test better and the day of his departure was a day of 'Hiraeth' [longing], so circumspect yet natural was his behaviour, so unfailing his courtesy, so remarkable his ease towards the most exalted of his visitors.'[18]

< V Press coverage

People who met him were often astonished at his relaxed humour at home and in some of the revival meetings.

Mr Roberts ... added that some of the people wondered why they laughed and were happy at these meetings. Well, who should be happy except those who had the love in their hearts. Before he got to his present state of mind, he used to take a serious view of all things. If they saw him laugh oftener than once in three months in those days it would have been a matter of surprise; but he laughed very frequently now, and he looked at the matter from this point of view; would a father be offended when his child laughed? No, certainly not; And they were children in their father's house—happy and joyous—and their father would not be, and was not, offended.[19]

Nantlais Williams, a young minister, newly converted in the first weeks of the revival, spoke of his first meeting with the revivalist at Evan Roberts' lodgings in Aberdulais. He was immediately impressed by Evan Roberts' natural, homely humour, his transparent sincerity, and his lack of any dour superspirituality.

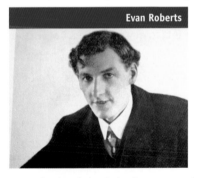
Evan Roberts

And that's not all; spending time with him that Monday in January 1905, he saw in Evan a depth of spiritual power that moved him deeply.

We all went after him. At last we saw him in the distance, standing on a rock, his back toward us, his arms thrown wide open. Anxiously and slowly we moved towards him. but eventually he turned towards us and when he saw us he smiled and that smile lit up his face and he greeted us welcomingly.

A minister from Ireland was one of our group and he had the first opportunity to present his concerns. 'I come from Ireland, Mr Roberts,' he said, 'and we would be very glad if you can come over to help us.'

At this Evan closed his eyes in prayer and said, 'No. I am sorry, I cannot come.'

'Well, said the man, 'can you recommend somebody else?'

He closed his eyes again and in a little while answered, 'No, but whoever you have must be firm as the rock, filled with the Spirit.'

He offered the last two phrases with thrilling passion. He was standing on the rock at the time; while looking at us he shot forth these words 'firm as the rock' and we felt electricity from him shaking us when he said 'filled with the Spirit'. We returned to the village all together and then went our separate ways. But I was invited by him to his lodging and we had a memorable talk sitting by the fire. It was as though he was filled with a kind of boyish zest mixed with the new wine of the Holy Spirit.[20]

There may be many reasons for seeing Evan as a central figure in the revival, yet this more than any lies at the root of it all—a personality filled with the Spirit of God. The Spring of 1904 had brought a closer intimacy in his relationship with God. But it is certainly at Blaenannerch on Thursday 29 September that Evan receives the power to accomplish the ministry that God is calling him to undertake. He is a different person after this. Out of the experience emerges the revivalist; the quiet student becomes an energised and envisioned messenger. He himself noted the change.

> **IT WAS AS THOUGH HE WAS FILLED WITH A KIND OF BOYISH ZEST MIXED WITH THE NEW WINE OF THE HOLY SPIRIT.**

I was having great pleasure with the work before, but now I am having the most pure joy on earth. And, oh I cannot say how happy I feel, because God works so powerfully on me, and has worked powerfully on me of late, and especially at Blaenannerch.[21]

However much the experience of youth and early adulthood actively influenced Evan, he himself saw Blaenannerch as a new starting point in his experience, one that was going to colour the message and direction of the whole revival. This was sometimes mistaken for his conversion experience by reporters. This bending to the Divine Will was the spark that lit the revival fire in the soul of Evan Roberts, causing an inner spiritual eruption that was to lead to a nation ablaze in a few months.

Throughout his short public ministry, this experience was to be a recurring theme. Preaching at Blaencwm, Treorchy, on 1 December 1904, he said

When God comes to bend us it will be awful. When God bends in His grace we are in the dark for a time, but light soon appears. I remember, while at Blaenannerch we were bent, but it was the hand of love that was bending us. We prayed, 'Bend us, Lord, bend us; Oh bend us for Thy Son's sake', and we were bent and made so obedient, that we ever do all that He desires. If you know what it means to be bent by grace, you would have an idea what bending in wrath can be.[22]

As he said in a letter to his sister Mary a day later, 'Last Thursday's meeting was the most awe full, and pleasant day of my life'.[23] And people noticed the power.

> Perhaps the greatest mystery of the whole movement at present is that the central figure of the revival, Mr Evan Roberts, is not gifted with a remarkable eloquence which is generally the attribute of a man who sways multitudes. As I heard a man remark ... 'We have plenty of better speakers and possibly abler men, but they do not seem to be imbued with the same power as he wields in drawing these immense crowds and keeping them together. At present I can only account for the fact that he comes from the midst of the Loughor fire.'[24]

Evan Roberts' message on the Holy Spirit's enabling power also came directly from his personal experience at Blaenannerch. His definition and explanation of the 'baptism of the Spirit' was a retelling of the story of his own empowering. This brought strength, conviction and authority to his message. It was more than theory. He wasn't seeking to prove a certain brand of Holy Spirit theology. He was simply, passionately excited about what the Holy Spirit could do in people's lives. Of course, due to his subjective understanding of his experience, there was a tendency to expect others to respond in exactly the same way. And when they didn't, it led Evan to an increased frustration.

> **HE WAS SIMPLY, PASSIONATELY EXCITED ABOUT WHAT THE HOLY SPIRIT COULD DO IN PEOPLE'S LIVES.**

This probably gives us a clue to understanding his harshness in certain revival meetings. Having little patience with the shallowness and curiosity-filled public, he often reproved congregations when he felt the entertainment element was taking over. Being entertained, for him, was not an element of Christian worship. To such a soul as Roberts, worship services were an opportunity for divine encounters, resulting in salvation and transformation in morals and character. They were not opportunities for endless hymn-singing, emotional indulgence or self-glorifying testimony. His message was 'away with self', the glory must go to God—a lesson he himself was having to constantly learn.

Evan Roberts' empowering had a purpose, of which he had been aware of for years, but one that he had kept secret.

> For years I have known I was to be the means of bringing about a revival in Wales, but I have kept it a secret, it will spread throughout the world.[25]

A work colleague who spoke about the possibility of revival to Evan three or four years previous to the awakening remembered him describing his desire to see a revivalist coming out of Loughor: 'One like Paul, till the place is on fire.' When Evan returned to Loughor in October 1904 he was reminded of that conversation at the coal face and responded, 'I knew at that time that  I was to be one of them'.[26]

This sense of being called to do the work of reviving a nation was confirmed to Evan by a series of visions that he experienced during his time at Newcastle Emlyn and the first few weeks of revival at Loughor. Visions of hell's doors being closed for a year, pictures of Satan's defeat at the hand of Christ, a cheque with the number 100,000 written on it, the light of a candle being overtaken by the light of the sun ... promises and confirmation to Evan of what was going to happen soon in Wales. He often shared these visions in the meetings.

It was a few Sundays ago at Newcastle Emlyn. For days he had been brooding over the apparent failure of modern Christian agencies; and he felt wounded in the spirit that the Church of God should so often be attacked. While in this Slough of Despond he walked in the garden. It was about 4.00pm. Suddenly, in the hedge on his left, he saw a face full of scorn, hatred and derision and heard defiance. It was the Prince of this World, who exulted in his despondency. Then there suddenly appeared another figure, gloriously arrayed in white, bearing in hand a flaming sword borne aloft. The sword fell athwart the first figure, and it instantly disappeared. He could not see the face of the sword bearer. 'Do you not see the moral?' queried the missioner with face beaming with delight. 'Is it not the Church of Christ is to be triumphant? ... It was a distinct vision. There was no mistake. And full of the promise which that vision conveyed, I went to Loughor, and from Loughor to Aberdare, and from Aberdare to Pontycymmer.

And what do I see? The promise literally fulfilled. The sword is descending on all hands, and Satan is put to flight. Amen.'[27]

However one might interpret these visions today—whether as the sanctified dreams of an overactive imagination or the immediate revelation of a sovereign Lord—one cannot get away from the fact that a few weeks after they had been experienced they were in the process of being fulfilled—and being fulfilled partly through the visionary himself! He had known that God had called him to do something extraordinary for years. He had just been waiting for the power to do it, and it came at Blaenannerch.

All these elements—his contrasting style, the controversy surrounding him, his engaging character and his sense of being called to the work—help explain why Evan Roberts became and is still seen as the central character of the 1904 Welsh Revival. Yet to get a fuller picture we need to note the challenge he presented.

Evan Roberts was not interested in emotional fervour for its own sake. He wasn't even interested in full churches for the Church's sake. His passion was to see God glorified through the transformation of individuals. He longed for a pure nation of transformed people, yet he realised that to achieve this—to see national revival—would involve personal cost to those individuals. It's a cost he had paid. He'd been through his own bending experience but it was an experience that led to the joyful resurrection of his soul, and he was passionate to encourage others to take a similar road. A road of pain before power, of a cross before a crown, and of a struggle before a victory. The cerebral and conventional Christianity of early-twentieth-century Wales was confronted by the dynamic, experiential 'charismatic' Christianity of Evan Roberts.

> **HIS PASSION WAS TO SEE GOD GLORIFIED THROUGH THE TRANSFORMATION OF INDIVIDUALS. HE LONGED FOR A PURE NATION OF TRANSFORMED PEOPLE ...**

The four points so prominent in the early weeks and months of his public revival ministry bring into focus the steps he felt Christians had to take in order to experience renewal. Dealing with all things doubtful and being willing to obey the promptings of God's Spirit challenged church members to act on what they believed to be true. Evan brought no new theology; he simply shared the way people could experience what they already believed by taking certain practical steps.

When confronted by the challenge, many stalled at the starting line as they contemplated the cost of their move. Some were frightened or upset and took steps back, but hundreds of faithful and not-so-faithful churchgoers took the plunge and experienced the consequence: a fresh assurance and boldness in their faith.

At times it's possible that Evan Roberts himself did a little too much pushing. He found it hard to understand that anyone would eventually not take the step from mental ascent to active living obedience, a step that had totally transformed his life. Evan was convinced that the way to national revival was through the Church, and the way to revive the Church was through the individual. He realised that God was not looking for new methods primarily, but for new people, as Tozer said many years later. He consequently saw that new people often needed new methods or, as Jesus put it, 'New wine into new wineskins' (Matt. 9:17).

> **EVANS WAS CONVINCED THAT THE WAY TO NATIONAL REVIVAL WAS THROUGH THE CHURCH, AND THE WAY TO REVIVE THE CHURCH WAS THROUGH THE INDIVIDUAL.**

But new people does not mean perfect people—and although some writers have tended to see Evan Roberts through 'sin-filtering glasses' the reality of the matter is that like all believers—famous or not—he was very human and fallible. He made his mistakes, he overemphasised some things at the expense of other things. At times he was too harsh and said too much. At other times he just said too little. He was often accurate in the way he discerned situations and congregations, but he also got it wrong, as each of us does.

Perhaps it's here, in his imperfection, that the greatest challenge lies to Christians today, for the story of Evan Roberts doesn't let imperfect people off the hook of commitment. Rather, it highlights the fact that God has used and can use people who still have a lot to learn. An element of naïvety and imbalance does not stop God using those who are determined to bend to His will. There are no perfect heroes and no sinless saints, and God's continued act of deliverance will still come through a tainted 'crowd of witnesses' who are determined and willing to count the cost for a lost world.

# POSTSCRIPT

The toll and strain of revival meetings eventually caught up with Evan Roberts in the autumn of 1906. After the Llandindrod Convention in the summer of that year, he was taken in by Mr and Mrs Jessie Penn Lewis at Leicester so that he could have 'time out' to recover mentally and physically. It was said that he was 'unable to stand or walk for almost a twelvemonth'.[1]

By the spring of 1909 he was feeling well enough to begin to work on what he felt God was calling him to do, and during the next few years he was to be involved in the publication of a new Christian magazine, *The Overcomer*, besides being co-author of a book on spiritual warfare, *War on the Saints*. He also gave time to encouraging Christian workers through conference talks and letters but, more than all these, he felt a call to intercessory prayer. Writing in about 1909, he noted; 'Since I have been fully given to prayer, it is marvellous how the world, the whole world, has become a sphere of vision to me ... Oh how sweet it was to gather the whole world under the wings of my prayers'.[2]

In the early 1920s, Evan moved to Brighton where he continued to write a few pamphlets. In the late 1920s he returned to the Loughor area and was involved in a number of enthusiastic revival meetings at the Old Post Office, Gorseinon. These had been organised partly by Mary Davies who had been one of his soloists during the revival years.

After these meetings Evan Roberts retired from the public gaze, living the rest of his life in Cardiff. He continued to keep contact with many of his revival colleagues and also continued to write his poetry, most of which still remains unpublished. These poems give much insight into his thoughts and feelings in the latter part of his life, and need further study. Evan never married and, as far as we know, never sought to marry.

Evan Roberts died in January 1951 at 72 years of age, beloved and remembered by thousands who had experienced renewal through his message.[3]

Evan Roberts' striking message

There is no question of creed or of dogma in this movement. The work that is being done has the support, I believe, of all church people and Christian churches in our country. I have merely preached the religion of Jesus that I myself have experienced.

God has 'made me glad' and I am showing others the great joy of seeing Him, a joy so great and so wonderful that I shall never be able to express it in its completeness. We are teaching no sectarian doctrine—only the wonder and beauty of Christ's love, the love of man for Him and the love of man for man. I have been asked too concerning my methods. I have none. I never prepare the words I shall speak, I leave all that to Him. I am not the source for this revival. I am only one agent in what is growing to be a multitude. I am not moving men's hearts and changing men's lives; not I, but God working in me. I have found what is, in my belief, the highest kind of Christianity. I desire to give my life which is all I have to give, to helping others to find it also. Many have already found it, thank God, and many more are finding it through them.

This is my work as He has pointed it out to me. His Spirit came to me one night when upon my knees I asked Him for guidance, and five months later I was baptised with the Spirit. He has led me as He will lead all those who, conscious of their human weakness, lean upon Him as children upon a father. I know that the work which has been done through me is not due to any human ability that I possess. It is His work and to His glory ...

I desire nothing but to be allowed to continue this work that has been begun. The Lord is my Shepherd. I fear no want. All things necessary He has provided and will provide. I want no personal following, only the world for Christ!

Some things have been said about our meetings, and about me, which are not true; but God's truth has not been hurt by these mis-statements, and they therefore matter little. I believe, too, that He has put it into the hearts of those who have written of the revival to say helpful things, for some of the papers have carried our message to many whom we have not personally reached.

I believe that the world is upon the threshold of a great religious revival and I pray daily that I may be allowed to help bring this about.

I beseech all those who confess Christ to ask Him today, upon the knees, if He has not some work for them to do now. He will lead them all as He has led us. He will make them pillars of smoke by day and pillars of fire by night to guide all men to Him. Wonderful things have happened in Wales in a few weeks, but they are only a beginning. The world will be swept by His Spirit as by a rushing mighty wind. Many who are now silent Christians, negative Christians, Christians whose belief means little to them and nothing to anyone else, will lead in the movement.

Groping, hesitating, half-hearted Christians will see a great light, and will reflect this light to thousands of thousands in utter darkness. The whole world will hear this message of 'peace, good will toward men'. And listening will be blessed. Thousands upon thousands will do more than we have accomplished as God gives them power. This is my earnest faith, if the churches will learn the great lesson of obedience to the voice of the Holy Spirit. Obedience! Obedience! Obedience![4]

NOTES
CHAPTER 1
1.   George Jones, 'Angen Cymru am Ddiwyigiad Crefyddol', *Drysorfa,* November 1902, p.508.

2.   'Ad Gofion am Ddiwigiad 59 yn Aberporth and Blaenanerch', *Drysorfa,* June 1901, p.318; 'Un o Flynyddoedd Deheulaw y Goruchaf 1859', *Drysorfa,* January 1904, p.29.

3.   Henry Hughes, *Diwygiadau Crefyddol Cymru (History of Religious Revivals in Wales),* Caernarfon, 1906.

4.   *Goleuad,* 3 January 1900.

5.   R.B. Jones, *Rent Heavens,* London, Stanley Martin, p.32.

6.   Dean Howell, 'Wales' greatest need', *Y Cyfail Eglwysig,* December 1902; *Dysgeidydd,* January 1903).

CHAPTER 2
1.   D.M. Phillips, *Evan Roberts: The Great Welsh Revivalist and His Work*, London, Marshall Bros., 1906; eighth edition, 1923 (DMP), p.67.

2.   T. Francis (ed.), *Y Diwygiad a'r Diwygwyr,* Dolgellau, E.W. Evans, 1906 (DD), p.10; DMP, p.14.

3.   DMP, p.14.

4.   DMP, p.17.

5.   DD, p.12.

6.   DD, p.13; DMP, p.20.

7.   'Diwygiad 1904', *Qualiton* record, 1958.

CHAPTER 3
1.   *Western Mail Revival Report,* vol. 3, p.30.

2.   *Chronicle,* February 1905, p.47.

3.   T. Francis (ed.), *Y Diwygiad a'r Diwygwyr,* Dolgellau, E.W. Evans, 1906 (DD), p.31.

4.   D.M. Phillips, *Evan Roberts: The Great Welsh Revivalist and His Work,* London, Marshall Bros., 1906; eighth edition, 1923, p.65.

5.   DD, p.19.

CHAPTER 4
1.   T. Francis (ed.), *Y Diwygiad a'r Diwygwyr,* Dolgellau, E.W. Evans, 1906 (DD), pp.35–36.

2.   *Llanelli Mercury,* 8 December 1904.

3.   D.M. Phillips, *Evan Roberts: The Great Welsh Revivalist and His Work,* London, Marshall Bros., 1906; eighth edition, 1923 (DMP), p.45.

4.   *Llanelli and County Guardian,* 17 November 1904.

5.   DD, p.33.

6. DMP, p. 93.

7. DMP, pp. 93–95.

8. *Western Mail Revival Report,* vol. 3, p.29; W.T. Stead, *The Revival in the West,* 1905, p. 42, combined accounts

9. Sydney Evans and Gomer M. Roberts, *Cyfrol Goffa Diwygiad* 1904–1905, 1954 (CGD), p. 33.

10. CGD, p. 36.

11. CGD, p. 34.

12. CGD, p. 35.

13. DD, p. 53.

14. R.B. Jones, *Rent Heavens* (RBJ), London, Stanley Martin, p. 23.

15. T. Mardy Rees, *Seth and Frank Joshua*, Wrexham, Principality Press, 1926, p. 71.

16. J. J. Morgan, *Cofiant Evan Phillips*, published by his family, 1930, p.330.

CHAPTER 5

1. Recorded interview, Aneurin Talfan Davies, 'Diwygiad 1904', *Qualiton* record.

2. William Morris (ed.), *Ysgolion a Cholegau Methodistiaid Calfinaidd (y rhai a gaewyd) (Memoirs of D.J. Evans)*, Llyfrfai, M.C. Caernarfon, 1973; *Qualiton* record, Chapter 1, 'Atgofion am Ysgol Emlyn'.

3. W.T. Stead, *The Revival in the West*, 1905 (WTS), p.44.

4. J.J. Morgan, *Cofiant Evan Phillips*, published by his family, 1930 (JJM), p.330.

5. JJM, p.41.

6. J.H. Howard, *Winding Lanes*, Cal. Meth. Printing Works, Caernarfon (n.d.), p.80.

7. JJM, p.199.

8. JJM, p.200.

9. JJM, p.169.

10. JJM, p.196.

11. JJM, p.332.

12. JJM, p.330.

13. JJM, p.332.

14. JJM, p.56.

15. DMP, pp.134–135, letter to sister, 30 September 1904.

16. DMP, pp.134–135, letter to sister, 30 September 1904.

17. Howell Williams, *The Romance of the Forward Movement*, (n.d.), p.172.

18. See Geraint Fielder, *Grace, Grit and Gumption*, Christian Focus, Evangelical Movement of Wales, 2000 (GF) for more details.

19. T. Mardy Rees, *Seth and Frank Joshua*, Wrexham, Principality Press, 1926 (MR), p.77.

20. GF, p.116.

21. *Weston Mail Revival Report (WMRR)*, vol. 3, p.31.
22. MR, p.73.
23. MR, p.73.
24. MR, p.74.
25. DMP, p.121.
26. DMP, pp.121–122; *WMRR*, vol. 3, p.30.
27. MR, p.74.
28. DMP, 85–86.
29. DMP, p.122; *WMRR*, vol. 3, p.30.
30. *WMRR*, vol. 3, p.30.
31. MR, p.74.
32. B.p.Jones, *King's Champions!*, Love and Malcomson, 1968 (KC), p.39.
33. KC, p.10.
34. *Drysorfa*, 1963, p.133.
35. *Drysorfa*, 1905, p.250.
36. *Drysorpha*, 1905, p.252.
37. *Drysorfa*, 1905, p.252.
38. Robert Ellis, *Living Echoes of the Welsh Revival 1904–1905,* London, Delyn Press (LE), p.53.
39. LE, p.53.
40. KC, ch. 62.
41. DMP, p.135, letter to sister, 30 September 1904.
42. DMP, p.134, Letter to sister, 30 September 1904.
43. *WMRR*, vol. 3, p.30.
44. DMP, p.123.
45. *WMRR*, vol. 3, p.30.
46. *WMRR*, vol. 3, p.30.
47. WTS, p.44.
48. MR, p.74.
49. *Llanelli Mercury*, 24 November 1904, p.6.
50. *WMRR*, vol. 3, p.30.
51. DMP, p.142; letter to Mr Davies, member of Moriah Chapel, Loughor, 11 October 1904.
52. DMP, p.132.
53. DMP, pp.132–133.
54. DD, p.56; DMP, p.137.
55. DMP, p.138; letter to Dan, 10 October 1904.
56. DMP, p.160.
57. DMP, p.141; letter to Mr Hughes, member of Moriah Chapel, Loughor.
58. DMP, p.139; letter to Dan, 10 October 1904.
59. DMP, p.138; letter to Dan, 10 October 1904.
60. DMP, p.139; letter to Dan, 10 October 1904.

61. DMP, p.141; letter to Mr Hughes.
62. DMP, p.138; letter to Dan, 10 October 1904.
63. DMP, p.142; letter to Mr Davies, 11 October 1904.
64. DMP, p.148, Friday 28 October 1904, letter to Sarah Jane Davies, New Quay.
65. DMP, p.156.
66. DMP, pp.159–160.
67. DMP, pp.156–157.
68. DMP, p.154, letter to Mary, 28 October 1904.
69. DMP, pp.152–153, letter to Mary, 28 October 1904.
70. DMP, pp.153–154, letter to Mary, 28 October 1904.
71. DMP, p.154, letter to Mary, 28 October 1904.
72. DMP, p.154, letter to Mary, 28 October 1904.
73. DMP, pp.155ff, letter to Mary, 28 October 1904.
74. DMP, p.169.
75. *Llanelli Mercury*, 2 February 1905.
76. DMP, pp.161–162.
77. DMP, p.162.
78. DMP, p.166; Letter to Florrie Evans, 31 October; WTS, p.44, combined account.
79. DMP, p.166; letter to Florrie Evans, 31 October 1904.
80. *Qualiton* record.
81. DMP, p.163.
82. DMP, p.167, letter to Miss N. Ceredy Evans, 31 October 1904; DMP, p.166, letter to Florrie Evans.

CHAPTER 6
1. D.M. Phillips, *Evan Roberts: The Great Welsh Revivalist and His Work*, London, Marshall Bros., 1906; eighth edition, 1923 (DMP), p.171.
2. DMP, p.220; letter to Sydney Evans, Wednesday 2 November.
3. W.T. Stead, *The Revival in the West*, 1905 (WTS), p.45.
4. DMP, p.221; letter to Sydney, Wednesday 2 November.
5. DMP, p.234; letter to Elsie Phillips, Saturday 5 November.
6. WTS, p.45.
7. DMP, p.221; letter to Sydney Evans, Wednesday 2 November 1904.
8. DMP, p.234; letter to Sydney Evans.
9. DMP, p.221.
10. DMP, p.234; letter to Elsie Phillips, Saturday 5 November 1904.
11. Version given to WTS. Evan Roberts seems to mix some details of the first week as he recounts his story to W.T. Stead. It's as if incidents merge into one as Evan explains the events of the first week.
12. DMP, p.220; letter to Sydney, Wednesday 2 November.
13. DMP, p.221; letter to Sydney, Wednesday 2 November.

14. DMP, p.234; letter to Elsie Phillips, Saturday 5 November.

15. DMP, p.221; letter to Sydney, Wednesday 2 November.

16. DMP, p.221; letter to Sydney, 2 November 1904.

17. DMP, p.220; letter to Sydney, 2 November 1904.

18. WTS, p.46.

19. DMP, p.224; letter to Sydney, Saturday 5 November.

20. DMP, p.235; letter to Elsie Phillips, Saturday 5 November.

21. DMP, p.235; letter to Elsie Phillips, Saturday 5 November.

22. DMP, p.223; letter to Sydney, Saturday 5 November.

23. DMP, p.224; letter to Sydney, Saturday 5 November.

24. DMP, p.242; letter to Elsie Phillips, Thursday 10 November.

25. DMP, p.235; letter to Elsie Phillips, Thursday 10 November.

26. DD, p.47.

27. DMP, p.236; letter to Elsie Phillips, Saturday 5 November.

28. DMP, p.224; letter to Sydney, Saturday 5 November.

29. DMP, p.238; letter to Florrie Evans, Sunday 6 November.

30. DMP, p.226.

31. DMP, pp.223–225; letter to Sydney, Saturday 5 November.

32. DMP, pp.234–235; letter to Elsie Phillips, Saturday 5 November.

33. DMP, pp.236–238; letter to Florrie Evans, Sunday 6 November.

34. DMP, p.226; letter to Sydney, Monday 7 November.

35. DMP, p.229; letter to Sydney, Monday 7 November.

36. DMP, p.244, letter to Williams the guard, Friday 11 November.

37. DD, p.59.

38. DMP, p.231; letter to Sydney, Thursday 11 [*sic*] November.

39. DMP, p.279; sermon at Blaencwm, Wednesday 1 December, referring to Evan's feelings on 8 November.

40. DMP, pp.231–232; letter to Sydney, Thursday 11 November.

41. DMP, p.239; letter to Elsie Phillips, Thursday 10 November.

42. DMP, p.240, letter to Elsie Phillips, Thursday 10 November.

43. DMP, p.244; letter to Williams the guard, Friday 11th November.

44. DMP, pp.240–241; letter to Elsie Phillips, Thursday 10 November.

45. DMP, pp.244–245; letter to Williams the guard, Friday 11 November.

46. *Western Mail Revival Report*, vol. 1, p.4.

47. *Llanelli Mercury*, 17 November 1904, p.7.

48. DMP, p.243; letter to Williams the guard, Friday 11 November.

49. *Ffydd ac Argyfwng Cenedl*, John Penry, 1982, vol. 2, Chs. 4 and 5.

CHAPTER 7

1. *Llanelli Mercury (LM)*, 5 January 1905.

2. *LM*, 26 January 1905.

3. *Western Mail Revival Report (WMMR)*, vol. 1, p.17, Monday 15 November 1905

[*sic*], Trecynnon.

    4.   *WMRR*, vol. 1, p.78, Tuesday 15 November 1905, Trecynnon.

    5.   T. Francis (ed.) *Y Diwygiad a'r Diwygwyr*, Dolgellau, E. W. Evans, 1906 (DD), p.273.

    6.   D.M. Phillips, *Evan Roberts: The Great Welsh Revivalist and His Work*, London, Marshall Bros., 1906; eighth edition, 1923 (DMP), pp.132–133.

    7.   *LM*, 1 December 1904, p.3.

    8.   W.T. Stead, *The Revival in the West*, 1905 (WTS), p.49.

    9.   *WMRR*, vol. 1, p.11, 18 November 1904.

    10. *WMRR*, vol. 5, p.25.

    11. Henri Bois, *Le Reveil au Payes de Gaulles*, Toulouse, 1906–1907, quoted by W.J. Hollenweger, *The Pentecostals*, SCM Press, 1972, p.153.

    12. *WMRR*, vol. 4, pp.4–6.

    13. *South Wales Daily News*, 16 March 1905.

    14. *WMRR*, vol. 4, p.25.

    15. Quotes from sermon of Evan Roberts, Llanlluan, 25 February 1906; published as a poster, 1906.

    16. *Cenad Hedd*, April 1905, p.118.

    17. Eifion Evans, *The Welsh Revival of 1904*, Evangelical Movement of Wales, 1969, pp.134–135.

    18. *Western Mail*, 'Evan Roberts as I found him', 16 February 1905.

    19. *WMRR*, vol. 3, p.6, Swansea, January 1905.

    20. An account of an event in 1905, Nantlais Williams, *O Gopa Bryn Nebor*.

    21. DMP, p.142, letter to Mr Davies, 11 October 1904.

    22. DMP, p.279.

    23. DMP, p.135.

    24. W*MRR*, vol. 1, p.7, Trecynon, Tuesday 15 November 1904.

    25. *Llanelli and County Guardian*, 24 November 1904.

    26. DD, p.17.

    27. WTS, pp.47–48.

POSTSCRIPT

    1.   B.p.Jones, *An Instrument of Revival: The Complete Life of Evan Roberts 1878–1951*, South Plainfield, NJ, Bridge Publishing, 1995 (*INST*), p.167.

    2.   *INST*, p.191.

    3.   For further details of the post-revival years, see *INST*; and Eifion Evans, *The Welsh Revival of 1904*, Evangelical Movement of Wales, 1969, pp.178–182.

    4.   *Llanelli Mercury*, 29 December 1904.

PICTURE CREDITS